D1453442

SZYMANOWSKI'S
KING ROGER
The Opera and its Origins

SZYMANOWSKI'S
KING ROGER
The Opera and its Origins

Alistair Wightman

With a Foreword by
SIR ANTONIO PAPPANO

Other Operas
No. 2

TOCCATA
PRESS

First published in 2015 by Toccata Press
© 2015, Alistair Wightman

British Library Cataloguing in Publication Data
A catalogue record for this book is available from the British Library.

ISBN 978-0-907689-91-1
ISSN 0960-0108

This publication has been supported by the
Anne Felicya Cierpik Fund
of
THE KOSCIUSZKO FOUNDATION
An American Centre for Polish Culture
New York City

Set in 11 on 12 point Minion Pro by Kerrypress Ltd, Luton
Printed and bound in Great Britain by CPI Group (UK) Ltd, Croydon, CR0 4YY

Contents

Illustrations

Foreword
SIR ANTONIO PAPPANO

The rare combination of ritualistic Christianity and total sensuality expressed in Szymanowski's astonishingly rich musical language makes *King Roger* an often bewildering and yet fascinating feast for the ear. The listener is overwhelmed by stunning orchestral writing of a very rare perfume which suits Szymanowski's style completely because of the often pantheistic nature of the text. But *King Roger* is much more than a world of ravishing sound. It begins – in one of the most arresting openings in all opera – in incredible darkness, as if the chorus has been singing that hymn for a thousand years. Paradoxically, it's the brightest strand in the choral texture which highlights that darkness: the sound of children's voices is always very disarming, and here (since what they are chanting is in line with the way things have been since time immemorial), it almost suggests, dare I say, brainwashing. That may be a cynical way of looking at religion, but I think it's what Szymanowski is trying to say. This entrenched and dusty status quo must be subverted and is, wonderfully so – at first. The figure of the Shepherd is incredibly alluring – he is Christ-like, in fact – and he brings an almost hippy-like message of love and peace, expressed in impossibly gorgeous music. But during Act 2 and especially that huge moment in the Second Act when he breaks out of his manacles, you sense the real menace and power of the character in a most disturbing way. It's the conflict of these two worlds, the tension between the status quo and the way things could be – the allure of change and the fear of what you don't know – that combines with questions of the nature of power and responsibility to give *King Roger* such tremendous depth.

Is *King Roger* opera? Is it oratorio? I don't believe it needs to be defined; it is a dramatic theatre-piece *par excellence* in the tradition of Greek tragedy, the chorus offering a commentary and bolstering the 'pull' of the piece. The central character, King Roger himself, commands our interest because of the torture he goes through, torn between conflicting impulses and the self-questioning they provoke. He reminds me of Leontes and his jealousy in *A Winter's Tale* – there's a very strong Shakespearean element to it, and Szymanowski must surely have been influenced by the ragings of Leontes. That Roger has to witness his wife being seduced by such a charismatic character as the Shepherd - to watch his partner float away from him – is profoundly unsettling and so makes very strong theatre. The use of tenor, baritone and soprano for the major roles is, of course, very traditional, but all is beautifully delineated, and every character is crystal clear; the role of King Roger's councillor Edrisi is particularly touching.

If there's a central message from the opera, it is in how King Roger manages (at least that is the hope; all is not crystal-clear at the end...) to embrace the positive in what the Shepherd is offering without losing his own individuality to it. What is clear is that Roger remains suspicious of him, and rightly so, since following the Shepherd's hedonistic message would certainly destroy him, and therefore he pulls back from the precipice. In essence, *King Roger* is the story of a life-changing wake-up call. At some point in life we are all confronted with a situation where we question everything we have previously believed; perhaps it's simply temptation – it could be many things. It's a very frightening moment – and for a king, used to the certainty of power, to being invincible, it could mean destruction. But if you survive that moment, you come out with a rare wisdom.

King Roger should definitely be in the mainstream operatic repertoire. It has a great baritone role and wonderful tenor and soprano roles and the chorus provides a ritualistic character to the proceedings and fodder for the Shepherd's message. It's short, too, which some consider a good thing! But it has a very simple problem: it's in Polish, and that's what scares everybody off. It's true that Janáček established the Czech language in the operatic world, but I'm afraid that probably isn't going to happen to Polish in the near future. Our production at Covent Garden is giving *King Roger* a good deal of exposure, and I am hoping that people listening to it will be really seduced. It's a challenge for any opera house, especially for the orchestra, but it's hugely worthwhile.

This book is an essential guide to Szymanowski's deeply disturbing but ultimately moving opera. I hope it will help elucidate, and therefore promote, this far too little-known work.

Introduction

Karol Szymanowski's *King Roger – Król Roger* in the original Polish – can be numbered among the most enlightened and illuminating operas of the first part of the twentieth century. It throws light on the human condition and radiates joy in existence – a remarkable achievement given its origins in one of the darkest periods of European history. Conceived during the final year of the First World War and developed when its composer was trapped in the Ukraine throughout the Russian Revolution and the ensuing Civil War, it was eventually completed during the difficult first years of Poland's independence.

In some measure, *King Roger* may well have sprung into being as an escapist creative reflex. Certainly, the exotic surface narrative of the opera at first seems far removed from its underlying message, and one of the aims of this book is to bring into relief the component ideological strands which informed Szymanowski's world-view. It opens with an account of his experience of the theatre throughout his life before dealing specifically with the writing of the libretto – in collaboration with Jarosław Iwaszkiewicz – and the music. There follows an investigation of the sources and philosophical strands which make up this rich ideological complex, which draws on Euripides, Plato, Pater, Nietzsche and, of course, various Russian and Polish writers, notably Tadeusz Miciński and Dmitri Merezhkovsky. The analysis of the music naturally sets out to show how the composer intended the drama to work, and the brief survey of the performance history of the opera inevitably touches on the increasingly fanciful interpretations which have taken hold in recent years.

King Roger works on a plane very different from those of conventional operatic models. On the one hand, it is far removed from the gritty realism of some works of the era, for example, Berg's *Wozzeck* or *The Lady Macbeth of the Mtsensk District* by Shostakovich; on the other, its elevated tone is in marked contrast to products of the jazz age, notably Krenek's *Jonny spielt auf* and the Brecht-Weill *Die Dreigroschenoper*. Its composition proved to be a difficult and convoluted process from the outset. No sooner had Szymanowski drawn up his initial plans than he found his musical creativity blocked, as he was caught up in the blood-letting of the post-revolutionary period. Consequently he turned to literary work, and in 1918–19 wrote

Szymanowski around 1913

Efebos, a novel which also touched on themes which appear in *King Roger* but which was largely destroyed in the course of the Second World War. Both novel and opera are concerned ultimately with the making of the whole man, with processes of integration which, in each case, leave its hero fully aware and in control of the forces which make up his very being. Reference is made to those extant passages of *Efebos* which throw some light on the argument of the opera, although it has to be admitted that in the novel Szymanowski, working in war-torn Ukraine, was not always able to avoid the lure of escapism, with the result that *Efebos* lacks the balance and control that distinguishes *King Roger*, one of his finest works.

Acknowledgements

As ever, I am indebted to Teresa Chylińska, the general editor of the monumental, recently completed collected edition of Szymanowski's music and editor of his correspondence and writings, for her invaluable help and advice in the preparation of this study. She has always been most generous in making available the results of her own investigations and in alerting me to the existence of ideological currents and influences not immediately obvious to the non-Polish student. I wish also to record my debt of gratitude to the late Wilfrid Mellers, who guided me through my initial studies of the work, and to Peter Franklin who commented on sections of the text in its initial form. Rosemary Lowther, PA to Sir Antonio Pappano in the Royal Opera House, helped keep the foreword on course. Finally, special thanks are due to Martin Anderson of Toccata Press who commissioned this book and who has edited the content with his customary care and attention to detail.

Alistair Wightman
Stafford
January 2015

I
Cast and Synopsis

Cast

Roger II, King of Sicily	baritone
Roksana, his consort	soprano
Edrisi, his Arabian adviser	tenor
The Shepherd	tenor
Archiereios	bass
Deaconess	contralto

Chorus

Act I: priests, monks, nuns, acolytes (boys' chorus), several dignitaries from the King's court, royal guards, Norman knights

Act II: women and young men (singers and dancers), eunuchs, courtiers, attendants, royal guards, the Shepherd's four companions

Act III: off-stage chorus

The action takes place in twelfth-century Sicily.

Act One

An evening service in a church erected by the Byzantine emperors, the former rulers of Sicily, has started. When King Roger enters with his court, he is urged by the Archiereios (Archbishop) and Deaconess to punish a shepherd who is leading the faithful astray and preaching about an unknown god. Roksana and Edrisi advise the king to hear what the shepherd has to say for himself. The Shepherd enters dressed in a goatskin, and tells of his god of beauty. The people accuse him of blasphemy but, to Roger's dismay, Roksana appears to be captivated by the Shepherd's song of truth and love. At first, Roger condemns the Shepherd to death but, in response to pleading from Roksana and Edrisi, orders his release. He again changes his mind as the Shepherd is about to leave and orders him to come to the palace later the same evening to stand trial. The Shepherd bids farewell, emphasising that it is the King himself who has ordered him to return.

17

Act Two

Roger, attended by Edrisi, waits anxiously on the arrival of the Shepherd. He issues passwords to the guards, and orders them to bring in the Shepherd when he arrives. Roksana can be heard off-stage begging Roger to show mercy. The Shepherd arrives, sumptuously dressed, with four companions carrying musical instruments. In reply to Roger's questioning, the Shepherd further alludes to his liberated world of beauty and love. The courtyard gradually fills with fascinated listeners, but Roger fears divine retribution for the Shepherd's blasphemy. The Shepherd commands his companions to begin playing, and the whole court, including Roksana, is drawn into a dance. Roger orders the guards to bind the Shepherd, but he breaks free and invites all present to follow him to his land of sensual delight. As he leaves, he tells Roger that if he truly wishes to judge him, he must follow him to his kingdom of sunlight. Left alone with Edrisi, Roger resolves to give up his crown and temporal might and follow the Shepherd as a pilgrim.

Act Three

Roger and Edrisi are seen alone in an ancient Greek amphitheatre in which an altar stands with traces of a recent sacrifice. Roger is in a state of uncertainty, having lost all faith and hope. Edrisi urges him to call out to Roksana, and her voice can be heard in reply, closely followed by that of the Shepherd and other distant voices singing in welcome. Roksana appears and persuades Roger to make a sacrifice on the altar. Flames leap up, and the Shepherd appears in an unearthly light as Dionysus, at which Roksana throws off her cloak to appear as a maenad. The stage comes alive with shadowy figures as Roger stands transfixed in the face of the Shepherd's summons to follow his call. With the breaking of dawn, the Shepherd-Dionysus and his devotees, including Roksana, vanish from sight and the altar flames flicker out. Edrisi realises that the chains of illusion have been broken, and Roger, acknowledging but ultimately resisting the power of Dionysus, climbs to the top of the theatre, and from the depths of loneliness, from the abyss of his power, offers his heart to the rising sun.

II
Szymanowski
and the Theatre

There are relatively few theatrical works in Szymanowski's catalogue of completed scores. His only full-length opera is *King Roger*, and even that is remarkably brief in playing time (it lasts approximately eighty minutes). His other major stage-works are the one-act opera *Hagith* (1913), and the ballet-pantomime, *Harnasie* (1931), based on the folklore of the Polish highlands. An operetta, *Lottery for Husbands* (1909), exists in complete musical form, but the connecting dialogue has been lost. There remain only a couple of pieces of incidental music: *Mandragora* (1920), composed for a production of Molière's *Le bourgeois gentilhomme* and *Kniaź Patiomkin* ('Prince Potemkin'), written for a production of a drama by Tadeusz Miciński in 1925.

It might then appear that theatrical music was only a peripheral part of Szymanowski's large output, but he always regarded himself primarily as a dramatic composer, although initially thwarted by force of geographical and historical circumstances. Born in 1882, he was brought up in the Ukraine, where his family owned property at Tymoszówka, a country estate in the Chehryn district of the Kiev province, and in the city of Elizavetgrad, situated over 100 miles to the south-east of Kiev. This territory had been subject to the Polish crown from the fifteenth century until the second partition of Poland in 1793; the Szymanowskis had arrived there in 1788, thanks to a marriage settlement, during the reign of Stanisław Augustus, the last king of Poland.[1]

The composer received his earliest musical training from his father, Stanisław, an amateur cellist and pianist described by a family friend as a man of 'deep musical culture and traditions, inherited from the home of his parents, where Tausig and Liszt had been guests.'[2] Subsequently Karol

---

[1] For further genealogical information concerning the composer's family, *cf.* Alistair Wightman, *Karol Szymanowski – His Life and Work*, Ashgate, Aldershot, 1999, pp. 2–8. *Cf.* also my 'Introduction: Szymanowski's Life and Thought' in Alistair Wightman, *Szymanowski on Music: Selected Writings of Karol Szymanowski*, Toccata Press, London, 1999, pp. 13–69.

[2] Bronisław Gromadzki, 'Wspomnienia o młodości Karola Szymanowskiego' ('Recollections of Karol Szymanowski's Youth'), in Jerzy Maria Smoter (ed.), *Karol Szymanowski we wspomnieniach* ('Karol

took piano lessons with his uncle, Gustav Neuhaus,[3] who also relayed to him an enthusiasm for German literature and philosophy, particularly Schopenhauer and Nietzsche. There was also much domestic music-making in the Szymanowski and Neuhaus households, the staple repertoire consisting of works by Bach, Mozart, Beethoven, Brahms and Chopin. One of the decisive events of Szymanowski's youth was a performance of Dargomizhsky's opera *Rusalka* by a touring opera-company visiting Elizavetgrad. Many years later he described it as the experience which 'decided the course of his life and destiny.'[4] It is also known that here he also saw performances of Glinka's *Ruslan and Ludmilla* and Weber's *Oberon*, but undoubtedly the strongest operatic impression of his youth was a performance of Wagner's *Lohengrin* he attended in Vienna in 1894. In 1909 he tried to explain to the musicologist Adolf Chybiński the extent to which this event had disturbed his equilibrium and shaped the immediate course of his life. He was acquainted with such works as *Faust*, *Carmen* and *La traviata*, but it was Wagner who became the 'sole object' of his dreams. He came to know all of Wagner's stage works from piano reductions, and emphasised to Chybiński that his predilections for the music of both Beethoven and Wagner were

> witness of my innate urge for symphonic music, and especially dramatic music, and that the role of piano composer was to some extent imposed on me because up to the age of 18 I knew *absolutely nothing orchestral and very little theatrical*. [...] I tell you frankly that at the first opportunity I will return to my dreams of music drama, as I understand it – and that only in that form will I attempt to express myself.[5]

There are, without doubt, many symptoms of that innate urge for dramatic music, even in the early purely instrumental works. The verbal musical directions embrace a range of human emotions – from *dolente* to *ardente*, from *amoroso* to *trionfando*. Further evidence may be found in timbral and textural devices, designed to heighten the expressive atmosphere – notably a fondness for intensely melodramatic tremolandi. Writing of comparable eruptions in the work of Schoenberg, Adorno referred to 'blotches [...], the

Szymanowski Remembered'), Polskie Wydawnictwo Muzyczne, Kraków, 1974, p. 32.

[3] Neuhaus (1847–1938) was the father of the Soviet pianist and teacher Heinrich Neuhaus (1888–1964).

[4] 'Karol Szymanowski', interview with Michał Choromański, in Kornel Michałowski (ed.), *Karol Szymanowski Pisma*, Tom 1, Pisma Muzyczne ('Karol Szymanowski Writings, Volume 1, Musical Writings'), Polskie Wydawnictwo Muzyczne, Kraków, 1984, p. 415; *cf.* also Wightman, *Szymanowski on Music, op. cit*, p. 335.

[5] Letter to Adolf Chybiński, dated 9 March 1909, in Teresa Chylińska (ed.), *Karol Szymanowski Korespondencja*, Tom 1, 1909–1913 ('Karol Szymanowski Correspondence, Volume 1, 1903–1919'), Polskie Wydawnictwo Muzyczne, Kraków, 1982, p. 175; emphasis in the original.

heralds of the *id* against the compositional will,[6] but in Szymanowski's case, it is just as likely that such effects simply arose from his treatment of the piano as a surrogate for the orchestra.

Szymanowski's compositional ambitions clearly expanded with his move to Warsaw in 1901 where he continued his musical studies with Zygmunt Noskowski and Marek Zawirski. His first orchestral work, the *Concert Overture*, Op. 12, was completed between 1903 and 1905. Its manuscript was headed by a quotation from 'Witeź Wlast' ('Włast the Knight'), a poem by Tadeusz Miciński, which promised 'a triumph proud and remorseless that covers the blue firmaments and shatters your powerless, pining gods'. Still more explicit evidence of Szymanowski's requirement for extra-musical and dramatic stimulus may be found in his first extant literary work, a prose poem bearing the working title 'Sketch for my Cain'. Dating from c. 1903–4, it comprises an outline of the content of an unrealised representation, requiring chorus and orchestra, of what the composer described as 'the first incarnation of the need for art in the human soul'.[7] In tone and language, it reveals close affinities with such writers of the 'Young Poland in Literature' movement as Miciński and Kasprowicz.[8] Furthermore, its translation of Cain from poor fugitive into artistic and creative lord and conqueror chimes in with the notion of the artist as a supra-human being, freed from the bounds of conventional society, as proclaimed by Stanisław Przybyszewski in his 'Confiteor', the definitive statement of Modernist intent, published in 1899.[9]

But by all accounts Szymanowski's dramatic predilections had revealed themselves much earlier. His sister, Zofia, mentions his writing of plays which balanced horror and romance, one of which involved the incarceration of a Princess Elsa in the castle of a German margrave: 'The frail golden-haired maiden, concealed behind the stage, had to groan painfully'.[10] Two of these plays became the basis of operas, now lost, performed by members of the family at Tymoszówka: *The Golden Peak*, written when Karol was approximately ten years of age, and *Roland*, completed at about the same time in collaboration with his brother Feliks, whose own compositional

[6] Theodor W. Adorno, *Philosophy of Modern Music*, transl. Anne G. Mitchell and Wesley V. Bloomster, Sheed & Ward, London, 1948, p. 39.

[7] Teresa Chylińska (ed), *Karol Szymanowsi Pisma*, Tom 2, Pisma Muzyczne ('Karol Szymanowski Writings, Volume 2, Musical Writings'), Polskie Wydawnictwo Muzyczne, Kraków, 1989, p. 78.

[8] The expression 'Young Poland' (*Młoda Polska*) was used to refer to a group of writers whose work represented a reaction against the materialism of the later years of the nineteenth century.

[9] Stanisław Przybyszewski (1868-1927), 'leader' of the 'Young Poland' movement had studied architecture and psychiatry in Berlin where he associated with Munch, Strindberg and Dehmel.

[10] Zofia Szymanowska, *Opowieść o naszym domu* ('The Story of Our Home'), Polskie Wydawnictwo Muzyczne, Kraków, 1977, p. 44.

style was likened to Franz Lehár's. It appears that dramatic presentations at Tymoszówka latterly became events of some sophistication. In August 1910, for example, one of their 'comic capers', as Szymanowski described it,[11] was a version of *The Ring*, with Karol's sisters, 'Nula' (Anna) and Stasia, cast in the roles of Brünnhilde and Fricka. Costumes and sets were designed by Nula, and Szymanowski provided accompaniment at the piano. The mounting of this performance was in itself symptomatic of Szymanowski's immersion in German music. He had attended Bayreuth in 1904, seeing *The Ring* and *Parsifal*, and throughout the first decade of the century had become acquainted with many more operas of all types. The deepest impression was created by Strauss' one-act operas *Salomé* – which he probably first saw in 1907, two years after its premiere – and *Elektra*, the first performance of which he attended on 29 January 1909 in Dresden, along with his friends Stefan Spiess and Grzegorz Fitelberg.

The impact of Strauss' work on Szymanowski was to become increasingly clear over the next few years, reaching a climax in the composition of his own one-act opera, *Hagith*, completed in 1913. Before that, he produced two very different works of a dramatic nature. The first of these, first performed in 1908 and subsequently revised in 1910, was *Penthesilea*, Szymanowski's Op. 18, a song with orchestral accompaniment. Though intended for concert performance, this through-composed single movement is quasi-operatic in nature, employing recitative and arioso as appropriate and showing some traces of Wagner in its harmonic language. It is based on an extract from *Achilleis*, a drama by Stanisław Wyspiański (1869–1907), and resulted from a commission from the committee formed to honour the memory of the recently deceased author and artist. In an intensely melancholy valedictory gesture, Szymanowski drew on the scene in which Penthesilea's dead body was briefly revived before being committed to the waters of the river Skamander.

The other dramatic work was the operetta *Lottery for Husbands, or Fiancé No. 69* (*Loteria na mężów, czyli Narczeczony nr 69* in the original Polish), a money-spinner started in 1908 with considerable enthusiasm. It was evidently aimed at exploiting the popularity of operetta in Lwów and Warsaw, and perhaps even Vienna. It was finished rather less willingly in October 1909, by which time it was hanging over him 'like a devil over a sinful soul'.[12] Written to a libretto by Julian Krzewiński-Maszyński, *Loteria* survived in two versions, one a full score bearing the pseudonym 'Whitney'

---

[11] Letter to Stefan Spiess, dated 7 August 1910, in *Karol Szymanowski Korespondencja*, Vol. 1, *op. cit.*, p. 222.

[12] Letter to Stefan Spiess, dated 14 April 1909, in *Karol Szymanowski Korespondencja*, Vol. 1, *op. cit.*, p. 178.

Stanisława Szymanowska as Fricka in the Tymoszówka 'Ring' (1910)

and the other a piano reduction. For many years the work went unperformed until in 2007 it was staged in Kraków for the first time, with a libretto specially devised for the occasion. In three acts with sixteen numbers, its orchestral demands are relatively extensive for a work of this kind, and in addition it requires a large number of soloists in addition to chorus; indeed, the sheer size of the performing forces may well have militated against immediate performance. It was also so stylistically sophisticated that one contemporary commentator, the composer Piotr Maszyński, father of the librettist, was moved to express regret that its

> beautiful, original melodies [...] enveloped in a delicate web of polyphony and counterpoint [...] and unusual harmony, so enticing and beautiful to the ear [had been] applied to so feeble a musical form as operetta.[13]

In truth, the savagely cynical tone of the work brought it closer in spirit to cabaret or vaudeville than the relatively genteel world of Viennese operetta. Indeed, it seems not far removed from Tymoszówka's 'comic capers', with their parodies of the 'Dance of the Seven Veils' (enacted by the composer's brother, Feliks, with Karol himself at the piano) and a thoroughly irreverent send-up of Gounod's *Faust*. There can be no doubt that, until the joke began to wear thin, *Loteria* provided Szymanowski with ample opportunities for amusement. Set in contemporary America, its grotesque cast of characters included the fat-cat, morally corrupt car-manufacturer Tobias Helgoland and his wastrel sons, Charly and Darly, Sherlock Holmes, Miss Huck and her Old Maids' Club and a band of Merry Widowers led by Williams, who is of the opinion that, however bad it may be in hell, it's worse on earth with a wife. Its action revolves around the setting-up of a lottery, open to unattached ladies of whatever age on payment of one dollar. The prize is a youth of independent means, so rendering the usual methods of match-making obsolete. True love eventually prevails, at least for one couple, though the work in general is characterised by both a vicious cruelty and scarcely contained cynicism. It has to be said that many of the texts are inconsequential and less than amusing, but Szymanowski nonetheless produced a charming score, with waltzes, quadrilles, marches and, perhaps more surprisingly, Brazilian machicha, cakewalk and references to 'Yankee-Doodle'.

As soon as *Loteria* was completed, Szymanowski embarked on a series of non-theatrical works which showed him to be the leading Polish composer of his generation – notably the song-cycles *Bunte Lieder*, Op. 22, and *Des Hafis-Liebeslieder*, Op. 24, as well as the Second Symphony, Op. 19, and

---

[13] Report by Piotr Maszyński, reproduced in *ibid.*, p. 167.

Second Piano Sonata, Op. 21. These works also confirmed that his general approach at this time involved an almost total immersion in Germanic styles and techniques. Both the Sonata and the Symphony follow a similar scheme of sonata-form first movement followed by variations which lead directly to a concluding fugue. When performed in major German and Austrian musical centres in 1911 and 1912, they were greeted with considerable enthusiasm by leading critics of the day, chief among them Richard Specht and Hugo von Leichentritt.

Yet Szymanowski was not quite done with his dreams of earning money from *Loteria*, for in 1912 he ordered a German translation of the libretto in the hope that a performance could be mounted in Vienna. In the end, the project came to nothing, and the work was never mentioned again. Instead, he found himself launched on an almost diametrically opposed operatic venture, the one-act *Hagith*, which would become his Op. 25. The idea for this work originated not with Szymanowski himself but his patron, Prince Władysław Lubomirski, who exerted considerable sway over the young composer. Lubomirski, an amateur composer whose other main interest was horse-racing, was a well-known, influential figure at the Viennese court. He had helped finance the Young Poland composers[14] for many years, and was largely instrumental in securing the post of conductor at the Vienna Opera for Fitelberg. He encouraged Szymanowski to sign a ten-year contract with Emil Hertzka and Universal Edition at the end of March 1912, and under the terms of a separate contract signed on 8 May that same year, he guaranteed a payment of 15,000 Austrian crowns a year for ten years in return for Szymanowski's rights and earnings with Universal.

Lubomirski's own three-act operetta *Die liebe Unschuld* ('Fond Innocence') was given at Vienna's Raimund Theatre in April under the pseudonym of W. Lirski, and rather than aid Szymanowski in his attempts to have *Loteria* staged, he urged him to compose a one-act opera after the fashion of Richard Strauss. It seems that under such circumstances Szymanowski could only politely accede to Lubomirski's proposal, and he agreed to use a libretto by Feliks Dörmann, who had provided the book for *Die liebe Unschuld*. Dörmann (1870–1928) was a 'modernist' poet and dramatist, and his libretto, drawn from a cycle of one-act dramas, published under the collective title of *Das stärkere Geschlecht* ('The Stronger Sex') in 1907, was evidently influenced by Wilde's *Salomé* in so far as it was an attempt to treat biblical source material in a sensationalist manner. But it lacks the sophistication of Wilde's play, and Szymanowski was aware of its

---

[14] Besides Szymanowski and Fitelberg, the Young Poland in Music Publishing Group also numbered Ludomir Różycki, Apolinary Szeluto and, latterly, Mieczysław Karłowicz.

shortcomings from the outset, asking Hertzka not to be too harsh in his judgment of it. It is a retelling of the last days of King David, the anointing of Solomon as king and the presence of Abishag the Shunammite (Hagith), introduced into David's household to lie with him 'so that the king might get heat'.[15]

Dörmann's reworking of these few facts requires a total suspension of disbelief. His 'Old King', on the point of collapse, is urged by the High Priest to draw strength and heat from contact with Hagith, a process which for no very clear reason will end in her death and his revival. While entering the palace, Hagith meets and falls in love with the Young King. They sing a passionate love-duet before he leaves to be anointed. Hagith refuses to comply with the High Priest's demands and the Old King dies. She is taken away to be stoned to death, and the Young King returns too late to save her.

During the composition of *Hagith*, Szymanowski worried both that his music would be far from popular and that the overbearing influence of Strauss would be painfully obvious. The resources required are huge, and as might be expected, there was a heavy reliance on leitmotif. Szymanowski made some use of *Sprechgesang*, and the musical language involves extreme dissonance, chromaticism, whole-tone writing and bitonality. Unlike Strauss' one-act operas, *Hagith* is relatively fragmentary and episodic, and avoids brutal naturalism, the depiction of Hagith's execution conveyed by way of a dissolution of the bitonal harmonies which marked her departure from the stage. There are also stylistic inconsistencies, most evident with the music of the love-duet ('Es gibt ein Herz') with its echoes of Puccini's *Tosca*, and in particular Cavaradossi's recollections of love.

Hagith had to wait almost ten years for its first performance (on 13 May 1922, at the Teatr Wielki, Warsaw), and it is not surprising that it has been infrequently staged since then. For Szymanowski himself, its completion became a chore, not least because he was becoming increasingly responsive to alternative creative approaches. He had resisted the allure of Debussy's *Pelléas et Mélisande* when he saw it in 1911, but the music of Stravinsky came as an utter revelation, as a consequence of which 'he began to hate the Germans'.[16] He was particularly taken with *Petrushka*, and studied all of Stravinsky's scores as they became available. Undoubtedly, his experience of Diaghilev's Ballets Russes – he attended performances in Vienna in January 1913 – opened his eyes to wider, unashamedly hedonistic theatrical possibilities. In his 'escapist' novel, *Efebos*, written in 1918–19, one of his

[15] I Kings, I: 1–4.
[16] Letter to Stefan Spiess, dated 14 October 1913, in *Karol Szymanowski Korespondencja*, Vol. 1, *op. cit.*, p. 394.

The first performance of Hagith, *Warsaw, 1922*

characters commented that the Russian ballet showed 'how to manage things in this field, and above all, introduce on stage that most beautiful of all things, namely a genuine youth'.[17] He was also strongly impressed by Franz Schreker (1878–1934), composer of *Der ferne Klang* and *Das Spielwerk und die Prinzessin*. He attended performances of *Das Spielwerk* in March 1913 and described it as 'most beautiful. Full of poetry and expression. In places the music is fabulous, and the instrumentation at times simply astounding'.[18] Fifteen years later, in the course of a fiftieth-birthday tribute to Schreker, he recalled that this work had been a 'startling, still vivid experience which I can see in my mind's eye even now'.[19]

In short, he became convinced that if, instead of *Hagith*, he had had another libretto, he could have composed something of real value. As early as late 1912 he began to think of writing his own libretto for his next opera. He talked of abandoning music for a while and going on holiday with only a notebook: 'perhaps some poesy will eventually be found to clothe everything in words and rhymes'.[20] In the short term, this idea came to nothing, but Szymanowski continued to accumulate experiences in different disciplines that would make their impact felt in *King Roger*. He had already spent time in Sicily, where the action of the opera is located, in 1911, and in spring

---

[17] *Karol Szymanowsi Pisma*, Vol. 2, *op. cit.*, p. 145.
[18] Letter to Stefan Spiess, dated 18 March 1913, in *Karol Szymanowski Korespondencja*, Vol. 1, *op. cit.*, p. 374.
[19] 'Franz Schreker zum 50. Geburtstag' ('On the fiftieth birthday of Franz Schreker'), *Musikblätter des Anbruch*, 1928, No. 3/4, in *Karol Szymanowsi Pisma*, Vol. 1, *op. cit.*, p. 226.
[20] Letter to Stefan Spiess, dated 24 September 1912, in *Karol Szymanowski Korespondencja*, Vol. 1, *op. cit.*, p. 356.

1914 he revisited the island and, in the company of Stefan Spiess, went on to North Africa. His memories of this expedition gave rise to the *Songs of the Infatuated Muezzin*, Op. 42, composed in 1918, and evidently stimulated a wider interest in Islamic culture as shown by the existence of three note-books filled with information on the geography of the region, the life of the Prophet, the Koran and Arab literature and science.

Before returning to the Ukraine at the start of hostilities in 1914, Szymanowski made his way back through Italy, and then went on to Paris and London, where he not only had the opportunity to see performances by the Ballets Russes (including Stravinsky's *Le rossignol*) but also to meet Stravinsky himself, with whom he considered himself to be 'on the way to an excellent understanding'.[21] But with the outbreak of war Szymanowski was confined to the Ukraine and Russia, where there was no realistic chance of performances of stage-works, whether new or already composed. For several years he devoted himself to the refining of the enriched mode of expression, characteristic of his 'middle-period' works, typified by both a heightened awareness of timbre and development of a delicate, sometimes 'orientalised' melodic style whilst retaining as a bedrock the high-tension chromatic harmonic language perfected in the pre-War years.

It seems that the impact of his travels in 1914 was immediate and intense. Almost as soon as he had struggled to find his way across Europe to Tymoszówka he embarked on the composition of his second set of *Des Hafis-Liebeslieder*, Op. 26. Unlike the first set for voice and piano, composed in 1911, this cycle is a work for voice and orchestra, and comprises transcriptions of three of the earlier songs and five new numbers. The orchestration immediately reveals a new-found sensitivity to instrumental colour and hints at forthcoming developments, especially in the exquisite final number, 'The Grave of Hafiz', into which a delicate orientalism insinuates itself by way of a juxtaposition of intervals of semitone and augmented second, a recurring feature in his melodic writing during the next few years. 'Mediterranisation' soon became evident in some of Szymanowski's subsequent works, notably the programmatic cycles *Métopes*, Op. 29, for piano, which evokes female characters from *The Odyssey*, and *Mythes*, Op. 30, for violin and piano, which draws on Greek mythology. Orientalisation is apparent in the vocal lines of *Songs of the Fairytale Princess*, Op. 31, and Symphony No. 3, Op. 27. Perhaps the most remarkable synthesis of old and new is to be found in the First Violin Concerto, Op. 35, composed in 1916, undoubtedly Szymanowski's most original instrumental work.

---

[21] Letter to Stefan Spiess, dated 2 July 1914, in *ibid.*, p. 441.

Szymanowski with Stefan Spiess (c. 1910)

In the early years of the First World War, Szymanowski remained close to Tymoszówka and Elisavetgrad, travelling no further than Kiev, but latterly he frequently visited Moscow and St Petersburg where some of his most recent smaller-scale works were performed, to acclaim from leading musicians of the day, among them Myaskovsky and Prokofiev. It was on these trips to the main centres of Russian artistic and intellectual life that he became acquainted with new currents in Russian drama, including the Chamber Theatre established in Moscow by Aleksander Tairov in 1914. Of particular interest in connection with Szymanowski's subsequent theatrical work was the staging in 1916 of *Famira Kifared* by Innokenty Annienski (1856–1909), a classical philologist and poet renowned for his translations into Russian of dramas by Euripides. Subtitled 'Bacchic Drama', *Famira Kifared* was a recycling of Orphic and Dionysian subject-matter in which the young hero regards the pursuit of music as the only aim in life. The gods permit him to hear music in its most perfect form in his quest for the secret of existence, but he experiences such raptures that he is left unable to distinguish between divine and purely human matters. Music played a vital role in all of Tairov's productions: incidental music was specially composed for each production, and frequently dialogue was intoned and movement systematically choreographed. The set, designed by Alexandra Ekster, operated on two levels, effectively contrasting calm and ecstasy, with

Aleksandra Ekster's costume designs for a Maenad (left) and Bacchante in Aleksander Tairov's production of Innokenty Annienski's Famira Kifared *in Moscow, 1916*

the higher level reserved for the Appolonian aspects of the drama and the lower the Dionysian. It is at least possible that this celebrated production, with its choruses of Bacchantes and dances and songs in praise of Dionysus, played some part in leading Szymanowski towards the formulation of the plot of *King Roger*.

The same year, 1916, also saw the establishment in Kiev of Studya, an experimental theatre under the direction of Stanisława Wysocka (1877–1941). Although Szymanowski himself was not totally convinced that Wysocka's productions were artistically sound, her theatre drew in numerous artists, designers and writers, including Szymanowski's cousin, Jarosław Iwaszkiewicz (1894–1971), who was to provide him with the basic libretto of *King Roger* as well as the verses which he set in *Songs of the Infatuated Muezzin*. Iwaszkiewicz was just beginning to establish a reputation as a writer, building on his early success with the novel *Ucieczka z Baghdadu* ('Flight from Baghdad'), published in 1916. It was a work which appealed enormously to Szymanowski himself, not least, as Teresa Chylińska has remarked, because of its 'oriental colouring and delicate affirmation of homosexual love'.[22]

[22] Teresa Chylińska, *Karol Szymanowski i jego epoka* ('Karol Szymanowski and his Epoch'), Musica Iagellonica, Kraków, 2008, Volume 1, p. 429.

Shortly before the Szymanowski family were forced out of Tymoszówka by the Bolshevik Revolution in 1917, Szymanowski completed his Third Piano Sonata, Op. 36, and First String Quartet, Op. 37. Significantly, he also started on two 'Greek' works, two settings for voice and orchestra of texts by his sister Zofia, devoted respectively to the mothers, Demeter and Agave. *Demeter*, Op. 37b, which he subsequently described as a sort of Greek Stabat Mater,[23] concerned the suffering of the goddess as she searched for her daughter Persephone. It was completed only in August 1924, at about the same time as the full score of *King Roger*. In contrast, *Agave*, Op. 38, was intended to evoke the Bacchanalian dance at the climax of Euripides' drama *The Bacchae*, culminating in the mother's murder of her own son, Pentheus. In the event, it remained uncompleted, its violent Dionysian subject matter eventually abandoned in favour of the broadly similar, but gentler, content of *King Roger*.

Indeed, for Szymanowski, composition in general became difficult during the Revolution and ensuing civil war. In 1918 and 1919 he completed only two song-cycles and three paraphrases for violin and piano of caprices by Paganini, this period of his life being characterised chiefly by a turn to literary work which he himself admitted[24] served as some sort of artistic surrogate. He focused on the selection of a subject for an opera, and at the same time wrote his novel *Efebos* which provides illuminating insights into Szymanowski's thinking at this period of his life and a fascinating commentary on the opera which began to take shape at the same time. And it seems that *King Roger* was by no means the only subject to be considered, as is shown by surviving literary sketches, dating probably from sometime after the completion of *Hagith*. One, scarcely developed, is *Don Juan*. It is impossible to divine Szymanowski's intentions here, as the remnants consist of no more than texts in French for two songs and a few lines of dialogue. The other, much more extended text, was intended to be the basis for a three-act comic opera on incidents from the life of Benvenuto Cellini. In some respects, the scenario recalls the scene from *The Marriage of Figaro* in which Cherubino is dressed up as a girl to deceive Count Almaviva. Here Cellini's sixteen-year-old servant, Diego, is similarly attired to save Cellini the trouble of finding a woman to take to a party. In Cellini's account, the incident is presented as no more than a joke, but in Szymanowski's sketch,

[23] Letter to Universal Edition, dated 12 April 1932, in Teresa Chylińska (ed.), *Karol Szymanowski Korespondencja*, Tom 4, 1932–1937 ('Karol Szymanowski Correspondence, Volume 4, 1932–1937'), Musica Iagellonica, Kraków, 2002, I, p. 160.
[24] Letter to Stefan Spiess and August Iwański, dated 17 January 1919, in *Karol Szymanowski Korespondencja*, Vol. 1, *op. cit.*, p. 571.

the artist's actions are motivated by a desire for revenge on his fellow-artist Bacchiacha for stealing his lover, Penthesilea.

> *Benvenuto*: [...] You know how that impertinent scoundrel Bacchiacca is susceptible to the charms of women. I should like to destroy his love for Penthesilea [...]. Tonight I will dress you beautifully. When the guests arrive you will bestow your glances upon him with a sweet smile on your lips. You will sing him songs and dance for him. He will be enchanted. The sweet wine of Italy and its fragrance will exert their magic. You two will stay together. When his loving ardour bursts into flame, when Penthesilea begins to writhe with malice and envy, I will come in with all the guests. You will throw off your women's clothes – and we will all laugh!
>
> *Diego*: Master, I am afraid of this divine game, but I will do what you ask of me. I am a little afraid that, in the midst of tonight's magic, I will be desirable.
>
> *B: (warmly)* You little Eros, there is no need to fear tonight's strange magic. How that divine emotion stirs in your little heart! But just keep completely collected. Just look at these rags. *(He takes clothing from the chest. Diego goes off into the apartment on the left. Benvenuto takes jewelry from a casket [...].)* You are becoming more and more beautiful, marvellous boy, combining in yourself the magic of a youth with that of a woman. Can it be that you are a beloved creation of Greek legend, immortalised at the hand of an old master? [...]
>
> *D:* When Diego the youth leaves hold of his sword, he forgets his manly pride. In woman's clothes he learns women's ways and appears before you here with new beauty. O Master *(half playfully)*, tremble in the face of feminine guile! *(He appears as a young girl, sumptuously attired.)*
>
> *B: (with the greatest admiration)* How beautiful you are!
>
> *D: (He stands still, conscious of his beauty, but embarrassed. Benvenuto approaches with the jewelry he has selected.)*
>
> *B:* The most beautiful girl is worthy of the most precious jewelry. *(Putting the diamond brooch in place)* [...] *(He moves away a little and gazes at Diego with the burgeoning joy of an artist)* [...] Oh, Benvenuto! Control yourself! Beauty is strong enough to subjugate the one who summons her.[25]

In the end, Szymanowski and Iwaszkiewicz between them settled on the 'Sicilian Drama',[26] *King Roger*. The sources for and writing of this work, and its links with the novel *Efebos*, will be dealt with more fully in the next chapter.[27] For the moment, it is sufficient to note that the initial sketches for the libretto were drawn up in 1918, and that it was revised and finalised in 1921. Composition was certainly under way by 1920, although the

---

[25] *Karol Szymanowsi Pisma*, Vol. 2, *op. cit.*, pp. 95–96.

[26] Szymanowski used this expression in the sketch he sent to Iwaszkiewicz on 27 October 1918, in *Karol Szymanowski Korespondencja*, Vol. 1, *op. cit.*, p. 562.

[27] *Cf.* especially pp. 41–71, below.

testimony of a Russian friend, Serge Puzenkin, indicates that Szymanowski may already have been thinking about the music as early as 1919 while still in Elizavetgrad.[28] The full score was completed in August 1924, and its first performance took place on 19 June 1926 in Warsaw.

The composition of the opera eventually became an exceedingly difficult task for Szymanowski. Confronted with the reality of the reborn state of Poland and the new-found sense of responsibility it brought, coping with the 'private' world of the opera posed particular challenges. Moreover, his musical style broadened to accommodate elements of the folk-music of the mountain region of southern Poland. Szymanowski finally moved to Poland on 24 December 1919, and immediately involved himself in the fashioning of a new song for the new Poland,[29] working tirelessly in a number of different disciplines. The 1920s and 1930s saw the publication of a large number of articles, many of which were concerned with the development of Polish musical and educational institutions as well as Romantic and contemporary music and the importance of a more enlightened type of artistic criticism. The first of these pieces, 'Uwagi w sprawie współczesnej opinii muzycznej w Polsce' ('Some Observations regarding Contemporary Musical Opinion in Poland') was published in July 1920.[30] At this time, Szymanowski was also composing orchestral marches and soldiers' songs in support of the Polish army, then engaged in a war with invading Russian forces which ended in late summer with Polish victory.

Earlier in the year he had accepted a commission from the Teatr Polski for incidental music for Molière's *Le bourgeois gentilhomme*. It was a noteworthy artistic decision, as he had previously avoided any involvement in 'utilitarian' composition. On being approached in 1910 by the distinguished novelist and dramatist, Stefan Żeromski (1864–1925) for music for the tragedy *Sułkowski*, he had refused on the grounds that he found it impossible to add anything to a poetic work which was complete in itself. He further discussed the problem he faced as a composer of incidental music in a memoir published after Żeromski's death, referring to the

> impossibility of attaining 'congeniality' – i.e., the fight for the right of existence between the existing power of the word and the just as great all-embracing immediate power of music in the unlikely event of my succeeding in creating something on a correspondingly high level.

[28] *Cf.* Chylińska, *Karol Szymanowski i jego epoka*, Vol. 1, *op cit.*, p. 539.
[29] Poland had gained independence at the end of the First World War, and Szymanowski was fully aware that he had to become involved fully in the creation of an appropriate musical culture for the new state.
[30] In *Nowy Przegląd Literatury i Sztuki* ('New Review of Literature and Art) and reprinted in *Karol Szymanowski Pisma*, Vol. 1, *op. cit.*, pp. 33–47; translated as 'On Contemporary Musical Opinion' in *Szymanowski on Music*, *op. cit.*, pp. 73–94.

The unacceptable alternative would have been

> to drape insignificant musical sounds over something which was in itself a complete work of beauty.[31]

With *Mandragora*, the final title of Szymanowski's score for *Le bourgeois gentilhomme*, the composer was absolved from seeking a solution to the problem of 'congeniality', since he was required to produce only a self-contained epilogue to stand in place of the concluding song Molière had demanded. Elsewhere, the director, Leon Schiller, used some of Lully's original music – notably the overture and a minuet – and also provided some of his own. Schiller, and his colleague Ryszard Bolesławski, formerly director of the Moscow Arts Theatre, approached Szymanowski with some trepidation as the composer had not previously worked to a deadline. In the event, the score was produced remarkably quickly and efficiently, to a detailed scenario drawn up by Schiller after detailed discussions with Bolesławski and Szymanowski. *Mandragora*, Szymanowski's Op. 43, draws on the conventions of the Italian *commedia dell'arte*, and is a charming example of the humour and grotesquery that typified both the home entertainments of the Szymanowski family in pre-revolutionary days and the earlier comic opera, *Loteria*. Set on the island of Huhubambu, it starts by depicting the plight of King Sinadab who is bored with his Queen, Gulinda; she nonetheless insists on performing a belly-dance in an attempt to rouse him from his torpor. A raucous parrot provides a running commentary, and the situation becomes still more complicated with the arrival of a number of *commedia* characters, notably Columbine, Arlequin, Captain Cocodrillo and the Doctor from Bologna, armed with his magic elixir, obtained from the root of the mandrake. Scored for a relatively small orchestra, with parts for soprano and tenor soloists, this delightful work is shot through with pastiches of waltzes, polkas and the vocal styles of early nineteenth-century Italian opera. It was first staged on 15 June 1920, and ran for several weeks.

Szymanowski gladly collaborated with Schiller a second time, on this occasion providing incidental music for a production of the drama *Kniaź Patiomkin* ('Prince Potemkin'), first staged on 6 March 1925 at the Bogusławski Theatre in Warsaw. Its author was Tadeusz Miciński (1873–1918), one of Szymanowski's favourite 'Young Poland' authors. He had already set several of Miciński's verses in two song-cycles (the Four Songs, Op. 11, and Six Songs, Op. 20), and the poem 'Noc majowa' ('May Night') had provided a programme for the First Violin Concerto, Op. 35,

---

[31] 'O Muzykę do "Sułkowskiego"' ('Concerning the Music for "Sułkowski"'), in *Karol Szymanowsi Pisma*, Vol. 1, *op. cit.*, p. 180.

Szymanowski at a rehearsal for Mandragora,
with Leon Schiller, Ryszard Bolesławski and Wincenty Drabik

in 1916. Miciński's influence is also evident in *King Roger*, which shares some features with the drama *Bazyllisa Teofanu*.[32] *Kniaź Patiomkin* was concerned with the mutiny which occurred at Odessa during the 1905 revolution on board the Battleship Potemkin. In Miciński's drama, these events formed a backdrop for a wider conflict between the forces of good, represented by Lieutenant Szmidt, and evil, personified by Wilhelm Ton. For this project Szymanowski was requested to provide music for the fifth and final act of the play, and the resulting piece for alto solo, tenor and bass chorus and fifteen-piece orchestra, his Op. 51, underscored the vision of the dying Szmidt. As distinct from the destruction wrought by the revolution, this final scene symbolised rebirth and moral regeneration, with priests in the palace of the Dalai Lama paying tribute to a child, described as the Little God.

Kniaź Patiomkin differs significantly in style from *Mandragora*, drawing to a degree on the modal properties of Polish highland music, and Szymanowski's final stage-work, the ballet-pantomome *Harnasie*, Op. 55, which occupied him intermittently between 1923 and 1931, was a celebration of the legends and music of the Podhale region. His interest in the culture of this part of Poland – the area to the south of Kraków – had been aroused as early as March 1920 by his friend, the musicologist Adolf Chybiński during a visit the composer made to Lwów for a concert of his works:

[32] *Cf.* also pp. 84–85, below.

The final scene from Kniaź Patiomkin, *Warsaw, 1925*

I could not let slip the chance to bring up the primitivism and individuality
of the music of the Tatra. One of the 'Sabała' motifs, played with a primitive
harmonic accompaniment of only two notes (bagpipe drones) caught
Szymanowski's attention with its particular tonal individuality. He asked for it
to be repeated. We went through other mountain melodies, but we came back
to it. I repeated this so archaic and, in its barbaric 'simplicity', so powerful
motive [...] with the thought that 'perhaps something will come of this', so
stubbornly did Szymanowski dwell on it.[33]

Throughout the 1920s and '30s, starting with the song-cycle *Słopiewnie*,
Op. 46b, Szymanowski produced a series of works, including the Mazurkas,
Opp. 50 and 62, the Second String Quartet, Op. 56, *Symphonie concertante*,
Op. 60, and the Second Violin Concerto, Op. 61, which drew on elements
of Tatra folk-music. This interest was by no means an abstract one. He
increasingly immersed himself in the mountaineers' life and customs,
spending more time in Zakopane, the capital of the region, and eventually

[33] 'Karol Szymanowski a Podhale' ('Karol Szymanowski and Podhale') in Jerzy Maria Smoter (ed.),
Karol Szymanowski we wspomnieniach ('Karol Szymanowski Remembered'), Polskie Wydawnictwo
Muzyczne, Kraków, 1974, pp. 124–25. *Cf.* also Wightman (ed.), *Szymanowski on Music, op. cit.*,
pp. 53–54.

Two costume designs by Zofia Stryjeńska for Harnasie *in Warsaw in 1938:*
highland man and woman

settling there, living at the Villa Atma from October 1930 until November 1935, when financial problems forced him to give up the lease.[34]

The scenario for *Harnasie* was drawn up by a Zakopane friend, Jerzy Rytard, in 1923. It consisted of two tableaux, and the first number to be completed was 'Pieśń Siuhajów' ('Song of the Highland Lads'), published as a supplement to an article on highland music and customs in 1924.[35] The first tableau was eventually completed by 1928, the second in 1931. A short interpolation was added specially for the production staged at the Opéra de Paris in 1936. In addition to a large orchestra with some extras (not least cowbells), it requires a tenor soloist and full chorus, and plays for approximately 35 minutes.

It was Szymanowski's aim in this work to make mountain music something that the 'good European' finds 'sympathetic and beautiful'.[36] Its plot could hardly be simpler: it opens with a celebration of the arrival of spring, symbolised by the leading of the sheep onto the mountain pastures. It goes on to portray a highland wedding, and culminates in the abduction

[34] The Villa Atma is at ul. Kasprusie 19. Since 1976 it has housed the Karol Szymanowski Museum.
[35] Karol Szymanowski, 'O muzyce góralskiej' ('On Highland Music'), in *Karol Szymanowski Pisma*, Vol. 1, *op. cit.*, pp. 103-108; transl. Alistair Wightman, *Szymanowski on Music, op. cit.*, pp. 115–25.
[36] 'Karol Szymanowski', interview with Michał Choromański, in *Karol Szymanowski Pisma*, Vol. 1, *op. cit.*, p. 422.

Szymanowski in Villa Atma, his home in Zakopane, c. 1935

of the bride by a band of highland robbers. Its closing number is a song in praise of the love of the robbers' leader for the girl. In some measure, this unique work acted as a means of preserving a culture in danger of extinction. It was, at the same time, one of Szymanowski's most significant contributions to the development of a Polish national style, and was in his own words 'a granite pillar which can never be knocked down'.[37]

It is a cause for regret that Szymanowski was unable to realise two other projects. The first, briefly considered in 1929, was to have been a comic opera – *Ewa spielt mit Puppen* ('Eva plays with Dolls') – with a libretto by the German writer and actor Alfred Auerbach (1873–1954). It involved a combination of contemporary themes with a number of characters from earlier times, notably Don Juan and Don Quichotte, the result being a parody of early Romantic opera.

The woman is completely contemporary, post-war, and at the same time a symbol of *Eve* (das Ewigweiblichen), flitting between these fantastic figures in the first act and finally discovering herself in dancing. A lot of truly v. witty and musically grateful effects. […] It would be light music, transparent,

[37] Letter to Zofia Kochańska, dated 13 June 1931, in Teresa Chylińska (ed.), *Karol Szymanowski Korespondencja*, Tom 3, 1927–1931 ('Karol Szymanowski Correspondence, Volume 3, 1927–1931'), Musica Iagellonica, Kraków, 1997, III, p. 456.

almost a chamber work, with intermezzi in a style parodying early operatic ensembles.[38]

Szymanowski evidently found the notion of a comic opera appealing, and as he tried to explain to Fitelberg, who had expressed reservations, Auerbach's libretto was ideal specifically on account of its parodistic elements:

> Something of the sort I tried to do on a small scale in that little ballet (*Mandragora*). Comedy attracts me and I've never had the opportunity to try it; and another thing, I cannot always be constantly so *ceremonious*, as in *Stabat* or *Roger*.[39]

Ultimately, Fitelberg's opinion played a major role in dissuading Szymanowski from proceeding further; indeed, he seems to have abandoned any further thoughts of composing for the stage. Remarkably, though, in the last few months of his life, when he was already seriously weakened by the tuberculosis to which he succumbed on 29 March 1937, he toyed with the idea of a ballet based on the return of Odysseus. The stimulus for this project was the creation of a Polish ballet-company which was scheduled to appear for the first time at the World Exhibition in Paris in autumn 1937. Following on the success of *Harnasie* at the Opéra de Paris, Serge Lifar (who had played the robber-leader) was persuaded to collaborate on the development of a scenario. Jan Lechoń, the writer and poet who at that time served as cultural attaché at the Polish embassy in Paris, was entrusted with drawing up the detailed version. But the task was never completed, and Szymanowski got no further than making a few preliminary sketches. When illness finally overwhelmed him, he abandoned work and the manuscript, which he presented to a friend, Iza Landsberger-Poznański, was destroyed at her home in Normandy during the 1944 invasion.

[38] Letter to Stefan Spiess, dated 6 January 1929, in *ibid.*, II, p. 23.
[39] Letter to Grzegorz Fitelberg, dated 16 January 1929, in *ibid.*, II, p. 47.

III
The Writing
of *King Roger*

The earliest sketches for the libretto of *King Roger* dated from June 1918, following extensive searches for a suitable operatic subject. Fragments from a sketch for a three-act opera on Don Juan, possibly dating from 1915, are preserved, as are sketches, in German, for an opera on *Benvenuto Cellini*.[1] Another possibility was suggested by Szymanowski's studies of the writings of Walter Pater. After his extensive European and African tour of 1914, he read both *The Renaissance* and *Greek Studies*, and in 1917, in the course of a letter to Jarosław Iwaszkiewicz, Szymanowski's eventual co-author of the libretto to *King Roger*, he referred specifically to the possibility of using one of Pater's *Imaginary Portraits* as the basis for a music drama:

> it was of course *Denis de l'Auxerre* [*sic*] I had in mind! It's a fabulous theme, isn't it?! And at the same time strangely close to me. But as for setting it to music – I have given up that idea for the present because of its epic character, the huge wealth of individual motives and the almost total impossibility of packing these into a dramatic framework. Yet I have not entirely abandoned the idea (unless I am deluding myself), since this figure is for me some sort of mystical symbol for various personal dreams about life – and it is difficult for me to part myself from him mentally. I should think this is comprehensible to you, since you must have guessed that I have a 'misogynist' view of life. I am writing about this to you with complete freedom and openness – since I like to lay my cards on the table, asking however that this bit of the letter remain your exclusive property.[2]

Szymanowski was clearly fascinated by the manifestations of Dionysus in this 'Portrait', first published in 1886, for 'Denys l'auxerrois' is the story of 'a denizen of old Greece itself actually finding his way back again among men as it happened in an ancient town of medieval France'.[3] Like the figures described by Heine in *The Gods in Exile*, however, Denys cannot fully unleash the powers of the ancient divinities. He wreaks none of the havoc

---

[1] *Cf.* pp. 31–32, above.
[2] Dated 27 November 1917, in *Karol Szymanowski Korespondencja*, Vol. 1, *op. cit.*, pp. 514–15.
[3] Walter Pater, *Selected Writings*, ed. Harold Bloom, Signet Classics, New York, 1974, p. 85.

associated with the Dionysus of old, his divine attributes evident only in good harvests in the vineyards, a love of music and nature and an intense joy in the dance. Distrustful of his curious powers, however slight, the people tear him to shreds, thus re-enacting unknowingly the ritual sacrifice of the god associated with the Orphic tradition.

Nothing came of the Pater project, and in June 1918 Szymanowski invited Iwaszkiewicz to Elizavetgrad

> to establish closer contact and to propose collaboration on a stage-work which would realise all his desires for sumptuousness and intellectual strength, for feelings, of which he was deprived and which could finally free him from certain religious, or rather religious-logical obsessions.[4]

Undoubtedly, the 'primary source' of the resulting Sicilian project was Euripides' final tragedy, *The Bacchae*, which Szymanowski and Iwaszkiewicz read together at this time. Iwaszkiewicz later wrote that the composer's attention was caught by one scene in which Pentheus, the Pheban king, was excited by the prospects of hedonistic experience in spite of his disdain for the Dionysian. The interpretation of this scene in Professor Tadeusz Zieliński's introduction to the Russian translation of the tragedy proved particularly influential:

> Zieliński noted the sensual agitation which drew Pentheus to the Bacchanalia, […]. In painting him a vision of drunken Bacchantes, Dionysus deliberately agitated the stubborn king and so led him into the trap. The sensual agitation and unhealthy interest displayed by Pentheus find their echo in the sensual curiosity that envelops Roger in all his meetings with the mysterious shepherd.[5]

Shortly after returning to Kiev, Iwaszkiewicz prepared the sketch of the libretto he had promised Szymanowski. This draft, the hero of which was not Roger II (1130–54) but the thirteenth-century Sicilian king, Frederick II (1194–1250), is no longer extant, but its content was later described by the author:

> Frederick II appeared in it and the black prince, or Arabian sage, to whom was allotted a significantly bigger role and bigger part in the action than to Edrisi in *King Roger*. [...] My sketch corresponded more or less to the present first and third acts of *King Roger*, for it lacked the Arabian second act together with the dance [...]. This sketch was only concerned with the initiation of the hero into the Dionysian mysteries, and the revelation of the eternally living Dionysus against the background of the ruins of the theatre in Syracuse

---

[4] Jarosław Iwaszkiewicz, *Spotkania z Szymanowskim* ('Meetings with Szymanowski'), Polskie Wydawnictwo Muzyczne, Kraków, 1947, p. 68.
[5] *Ibid.*, p. 79.

Jarosław Iwaszkiewicz in 1917

or Segesta. Of course the drama in this form had still less action than the present-day Roger. It was rather a two-part oratorio, half Byzantine church, half pagan. I sent the sketch to Karol in Elizavetgrad.[6]

Szymanowski's response was enthusiastic. Assuring his younger cousin that he was impressed by his 'uncommon qualities' and that they had an 'almost transcendental sympathy' for each other, he wrote of his conviction that their joint work could result in 'something of considerable importance'. He also tried to overcome Iwaszkiewicz's misgivings regarding the writing of an operatic work, and went on to elaborate at some length on the proposed scheme:

But unfortunately (or in my view, *fortunately*), the only terrain on which we could join forces for such a *definitive* work (and I don't mean a song-cycle for voice and piano – à propos of which I shall add a couple of words later), is precisely the theatre – a stage-work. Do not forget that music for the stage is a truly magical medium. It seems to me that you are not sufficiently aware of this for purely circumstantial reasons – namely, you have simply never had the chance to see a musical stage-presentation which was perfect in itself (Stravinsky, *Tristan* or *Elektra*), and are not conscious of this. Diaghilev's type of theatre, in spite of its perhaps numerous defects, offers something which in this respect is almost ideal in this direction, and it has opened my eyes wide to many possibilities. Unfortunately you have no experience of this!

[6] *Ibid.*, pp. 75–76.

Elizavetgrad

Returning to us, it is characteristic that the superficial Sicilian sketch which you sent me immediately enchanted me with its own strange immediacy; it was as if it became a manifestation of its own mystery! *I like it terribly of course!* And I should like nothing more than that you should begin to think seriously about it!

As a totally non-binding and external point, I only add that from the staging point of view (colour and group scenes, dances etc.), I would find a Byzantine-Arabian interior for the palace exceedingly desirable. Just think of it: tarnished gold and rigid mosaic figures as a background for Arab filigree, dances – what 'barbarian' opulence! Of course all this would be difficult to squeeze into a single evening. Perhaps two? Something in the style I've described (as a spectacle) – as a prologue to the drama itself (your idea) which then takes place on the true spiritual heights of real experience. Both connected by the central figure (Frederick, accompanied by the Arab sage). [...] At any rate I am now terribly enthusiastic about this idea and should like to instill some of my enthusiasm into you! Don't be worried at the absence of music – what there is (Pan etc.) will be more than sufficient. And (eventually) dark orthodox-Byzantine choruses!! Conceptually it more or less assumes the following shape clearly: huge contrasts and the richness of strangely related worlds (Byzantium, the Orient, Normans) (prologue). The search for the hidden significance of this, the solution of some insoluble questions (the drama itself – the theatre in Syracuse etc.). A quest in the midst of unheard-of treasures! I'm really becoming increasingly enthusiastic about this! In actual fact the scenic action itself (a plot involving some sort of woman etc. etc.) could be really rather loose! But enough of this for the present.[7]

Iwaszkiewicz replied to this letter within a week, telling the composer that he was increasingly keen on their Sicilian escapade, that many things were buzzing around in his head and that Szymanowski's letter had stirred up still more:

> I reckon those colourful elements which, if need be, you would place in the Prologue, could be placed in Act I. At the same time, Konstancja, the Norman mother of the King, could be placed at the head of the Byzantine-monastic choir. I am rather afraid of falling under the influence of Wyspiański's *Bolesław Śmiały*[8] with regard to the entire plan and language, but I will try to escape from it. In the last act, in the mountains, the conclusion will be a lullaby scene in which Frederick falls asleep in a cave to wake up many years later with a gigantic projection of the choir of the Queen Mother against the night sky. You know that this legend which is usually associated with Frederick Barbarossa (that is, the dream in the mountains), actually arose in connection with Frederick II? Do you like it?[9]

In fact, these rather fanciful elaborations never impinged on the final scheme of *King Roger*. For one thing, Szymanowski mislaid the letter after only glancing briefly at it:

> I feel awful about this, especially as you wrote something about our theatrical plans and I intended to ponder over them more deeply. Write to me without fail about *everything*. I should so like you to occupy yourself seriously with this. You have no idea how psychologically important it is for me, as in my present state I need some sort of external aid or stimulus – some sort of artistic insemination to enable me to undertake further artistic work. My isolation in recent years is beginning to weigh very heavily on me. This whole idea of a novel [*Efebos*] is some sort of attempt to escape from real life into what would be for me a suitable, fantastic environment – but in spite of everything it is only a secondary stream, to do more with the head than with true artistic emotions.[10]

This letter was written from Odessa, where Szymanowski spent part of September and October 1918, with his mother and oldest sister in the villa

---

[7] Letter dated 18 August 1918, in *Karol Szymanowski Korespondencja*, Vol. 1, *op. cit.*, pp. 542–43; emphasis in original.
[8] *Bolesław Śmiały* ('Bolesław the Bold'), a play by the Kraków-based dramatist and artist, Stanisław Wyspiański (1869–1907).
[9] Letter dated 24 August 1918, *ibid.*, pp. 545–46.
[10] Letter dated 18 September 1918, *ibid.*, pp. 548–49.

of their Russian friends, the Davidovs. Eventually he was joined there by Iwaszkiewicz who, acting as escort to Aunt Józefa Szymanowska, was able to undertake the journey to the Black Sea. There Szymanowski and his cousin sat on the sun-drenched beaches, discussing for hours at a time the most minute details of their theatrical venture. By the time Iwaszkiewicz left, it was decided that the drama should be divided into three acts: Byzantine, Arab and Ancient Greek in setting. The action itself was still not totally worked out, and so it was agreed that Szymanowski would draw up the scenario, while Iwaszkiewicz wrote the libretto, after which 'we were to merge things into one'.[11]

It is not surprising to find that in the long term this arrangement proved to be highly unsatisfactory, but for the moment Szymanowski at least forged ahead with the project, and on 27 October he sent Iwaszkiewicz his 'Sketch for the Sicilian Drama', which came to him 'one sleepless, "Spanish"[12] night':

> Included there are my personal commentaries as well [...]. But I should like you to write to me as quickly as possible with your sincere opinion of it. I believe that its anecdotal matter (the factual skeleton of the drama) is of rather less significance than its internal, emotional substance, so it seems to me that you can take my lucubrations into account either completely or in part without running the risk of being hampered or bound by them in any way. [...] Just one thing – I am so happy with the thought of working on this, so if at all possible, please don't disillusion me frivolously![13]

This remarkable document demonstrates that the action of *Pasterz* ('The Shepherd'), as it was first called (the title *King Roger* was adopted only in 1922), was almost completely finalised by this time. The one significant difference involves the very close of the opera, and in particular Roger's final, more ambivalent response to the Shepherd and the as yet missing hymn to the rising sun.

SKETCH FOR THE SICILIAN DRAMA
Main characters:
1. Emperor (possibly Frederick)
2. Woman (name? oriental? Wife or merely the favourite from the harem, in any case the love of the two strongly emphasised).
3. Arabian Sage the ever present companion and friend of the Emperor – providing so to say a philosophical basis for his deepest instincts.

---

[11] Iwaszkiewicz, *op. cit.*, p. 81.

[12] A reference to the world-wide influenza epidemic of 1918 to which Szymanowski believed he had succumbed, although he seems to have made a speedy recovery.

[13] Letter to Iwaszkiewicz dated 27 October 1918, in *Karol Szymanowski Korespondencja*, Vol. 1, *op. cit.*, p. 561.

4. Young Man (unknown)
(In addition, there may be other people essential to the action, e.g. the clergy in Act I – some old Archdeacon – an old man or several of them responding to the words of the young man, monks or nuns – figures appearing from time to time etc. etc.)

ACT I

Interior of a Byzantine Cathedral (Capella Palatina? existing to the present day and combining in itself the eternal Roman style, Norman and Arabic). Mosaics: dim gold – black Romanesque marbles – Carpets – Arab ceiling in form of brightly coloured stalactites. Shadowy – with glittering light of lamps and candles. Incense, thuribles etc. etc. Crowd, clergy in stiff, byzantine robes (as in mosaics) in cloth of gold. Severe splendour and rigidity with an oriental-Byzantine undercurrent.

> *NB. Basic tone of the music. Chorus – almost continually choral, a sort of liturgical chant, against the background of which the action takes place. NB. Action ought to begin with some liturgy – only later the entry of the Court and dialogue explaining the situation.*

Seemingly cold, but with a mystical, terrible and merciless fervour concealed in its depths. The court – a separate group: splendour now markedly Arab-oriental in dress and manner. The throne of the Emperor and his consort at front of the stage. Arabian sage next to them. Content of the exchanges: (perhaps an archbishop speaks to the emperor about this) has to do with the fact that that very day, before the Concilium there is to appear a mysterious holy-Anchorite-young man, or else a magician or simply a charlatan (the attitude of the clergy must be hostile and despotic towards him) living in a cave – to which people repair in crowds to affirm that he is a saint and a prophet, that he works miracles etc. etc.

> *Here one ought immediately to emphasise the hostile attitude of the clergy and the intense interest shown in him by the Emperor, his Consort and the Arabian Sage.*

The Young Man soon appears. Dressed in a white linen robe, with dark copper-coloured hair decked with a garland of ivy, a pilgrim's staff ornamented with flowers (a kind of thyrsis) in his hand. Marvellous, mysterious smile and sense of calm. The congregation stirs. Submission to his charm. A figure à la Leonardo da Vinci (in the Louvre). Either John the Baptist or even the young Christ, or the young Bacchus – it cannot be said for certain. Contrasts with his surroundings after the fashion of the young Christ facing the Sanhedrin.

To academic questions come replies full of charm. Best to have some song full of marvellous simplicity about God (Christ), contrasting with the gloomy splendour of the basic music.

The Emperor, the Arabian Sage and the Consort (the last especially with a characteristically feminine impulsiveness) visibly succumb to his charm. In contrast an increasingly explicit hostility on the part of the clergy. (Perhaps it would be a good idea to have some terrible old deaconess (alto) at the head of the order showing a fanatical hatred for the young man?)

> *NB. Technically the gradation of the feelings of these three is difficult – especially in the case of the Arabian Sage who, at this Christian ceremony cannot of course have anything to say and in the case of the Consort – who must however have something to sing, but it is possible to place this immediately before the outburst when she throws herself at the feet of the Young Man, so precipitating the catastrophe.*

(The Young Man's song ought to be a little blasphemous in an erotic way.)

After the Young Man has sung his song, the Consort throws herself on her knees before him in a state of transport, as if before a shrine. Uproar amongst the clergy (curses from the Deaconess), condemnation of him as a charlatan, a renegade. Emperor called on to condemn him to death or else imprisonment. The Young Man of course keeps calm and his mysterious smile remains intact. The Emperor, who is disturbed by the impulsive response of his Consort from a purely masculine point of view, is faced with the dilemma of fulfilling a vulgar desire to rid himself at one stroke of a dangerous rival and at the same time an as yet unconscious enchantment with the Young Man. The words of his friend, the Arab Sage, weigh heavily on him as he makes his decision. The Sage, who is also affected by the strange beauty of the youth, advises the Emperor to summon him to his court and there weigh up the matter for himself. The Emperor does this. The Young Man agrees, emphasising earnestly: 'Remember, it was you, yourself, who summoned me to come to you'. (Thus, in this symbolic sense, the Emperor by his nature to some extent unconsciously awakes in medieval times the Dionysian pathos of ancient life.) The Youth departs amidst mutterings from the crowd.

End of Act I

ACT II

Interior of the Emperor's Palace. Arabian décor – 1,001 nights. Perhaps part of the sky, with stars and moon as vista disappearing into infinity. By the doors Norman guards – huge steel-clad figures. I picture the set as a two-storey gallery-colonnade running round two sides of the stage (the third, e.g. the right side open to the heavens, with trees and fountains etc.) Besides this I imagine the upper gallery as being part of the harem, and there during the first part of the act the continual movement of women should be in evidence – whispers, voices, eyes glinting through the azure of Moucharaby – from this part of the set the Consort should perhaps have a song to sing. This second floor could be linked with the stage by an internal stair-case – so that at a certain point in the action a crowd of women, ephebes, eunuchs could make an effective stage entrance in their entirety. These are of course details to be considered.

Scene I. Emperor and Arab await the Young Man. Exchanges in which anxiety and the tension of waiting is sensed in the Emperor. Here also, perhaps, the Consort (out of sight in the upper gallery) could sing an aria warning the Emperor against harshness – perhaps it would be possible to repeat it a couple of times later, during the scene involving exchanges with the Young Man.

Scene II. Young Man arrives, this time in the marvellous garments of an Arab (or perhaps Hindi?) patrician. In any case he ought to be dressed in white (covered with pearls and diamonds) – which in the final scene should reflect the colour of the crowd. Perhaps he should have with him several suivantes – who could later provide music if necessary. Further exchanges, the tone of which is different. Here the charm of the Young Man begins to resonate in an increasingly disturbing way, with something subtly sensual and alluring. Something along the lines of the exchanges between Pentheus and Dionysus in *The Bacchae*. (The Arab could be absent.)

> *The increasingly submissive attitude of the Emperor should be emphasised.*

It would be good to have him sing some strange song. On account of this song, strange things begin to happen. All around, intense animation begins to be evident. On the steps and in the gallery, women begin to appear. The Consort, with her entourage, appears on stage and begins to gaze at the Young Man. The stage gradually fills with women, ephebes, the crowd generally hypnotised by the strange music. Here one should pass adroitly from the idea of song to that of dance. Possibly the Young Man could appear with a few courtiers who were also instrumentalists (everything of course in Arab mode) who initially accompany him in song, proceeding imperceptibly to the rhythms of the dance. A sort of frenzy slowly begins to seize the crowd – the movement spreads and begins to change into an orgiastic dance. At the centre of this is of course the Young Man, standing on a dais, looking with an enigmatic smile at what is happening around him.

The mounting frenzy in the Consort and the Emperor's divided feelings should be emphasised.

Finally, at the moment of maximum tension, the Consort suddenly throws herself at the feet of the Young Man, crying that she will go with him everywhere (or something of the sort). Here the Emperor still displays an element of ordinary, masculine instinct, commanding his mighty, Norman guards to imprison (or bind) the Young Man. All movement ceases for a moment.

The soothing voice of the Young Man is again heard, pointedly reminding the Emperor that it was he himself who ordered him to come. He then throws down his chains at the Emperor's feet (again an analogy with *The Bacchae*), and he slowly makes for the entrance, saying that whoever is free should follow him (there where... etc. – room for an aria). The Consort, hypnotised, follows him.

One ought to beware of over-emphasising the vulgarly erotic elements (perhaps the whole crowd should follow him?). The guards and the whole crowd part to make way for him. Before making his exit, the Young Man turns again to the Emperor, calling on him to follow, like his Consort.

The Emperor remains alone on stage in some tragic [illegible word].

End of Act II

ACT III

Night. Interior of Greek theatre at Syracuse. Stone semicircles rising one on top of another; above them thickets, cypresses. Sky above with enormous, glittering stars. On left, diagonally, the ruins of the stage, fallen columns, friezes etc. Centre-stage the altar of Dionysus. The Emperor and Arabian Sage enter in search of the Consort. Dialogue, in which one senses that it is not really about her that the Emperor is concerned. The Sage slips away to make a more extensive search of the grottoes, as it is there that the mysterious Young Man lives. From this point there are two possible continuations of this act: 1) After the Sage goes away, the Young Man appears clothed completely in a grey cloak. 'You have come to me... etc.' Third and final exchange between the Emperor and the Young Man in which the feelings of the Emperor become increasingly more clearly defined. The Young Man summons the Consort, returning her as it were to the Emperor and then vanishing. The next scene as in the second version after the arrival of the woman.

Version 2 (dramatically better since it avoids the repetition of the dialogue between the Young Man and the Emperor, and saves the appearance of the Youth until the end of the act.)

After the departure of the Arab, the Emperor remains alone for a moment (The Young Man does not appear at all). After a moment, the singing of the Consort is heard in the distance – she comes down from the top of the theatre, almost invisible, wrapped in a grey cloak, and slowly approaches the Emperor, singing some strange song. The two meet.

The Consort says that the Young Man has sent her to him, and artfully adds that if the Emperor wishes, they can now depart. Emphasis on mood of anticipation of something or other, in other words, although the Emperor has retrieved what, properly speaking, he came for, he is by no means in a hurry to leave, as if he is expecting something.

The Consort artfully asks the Emperor whether he wants him to appear and whether she should summon him.

Emperor is initially nervous, but then with increasing fervour asks her to do this! Dawn begins to break. Some strange power and exultation begins to burn more obviously in the Consort. Shaking the thyrsis she holds in her hand she emits the cry of a Bacchante. (Evoe – or something of this kind.) From behind the stage similar voices are heard in reply, initially one at a time, then slowly beginning to join together in a single choral cry. Frenzied anticipation of a miracle seizes the Emperor and his Consort. Dawn light begins to strengthen noticeably as voices are heard approaching. At one point the Arab Sage runs on stage, crying in highest exaltation that the God (or prophet) is approaching at just that moment. The Consort throws off her grey cloak and appears in the guise of a Maenad (Greek concept). On the steps of the theatre, groups of Bacchantes begin to appear separately. At last, on the highest stone step – or on the stage – clearly lit by the first rays of the sun, the Young Man appears in the form of the Greek Dionysus, surrounded by the orgiastic crowd. (I reckon he ought to say nothing.) The Consort by now has joined the crowd. The Emperor, crying out that he has seen 'God', throws himself at his feet.

> *End*

NB The flute of Pan must be a leitmotif throughout the whole act, perhaps appearing initially from the first cries of the Bacchantes, or even earlier – somewhere off-stage, betraying some intense form of life concealed in the thickets.

NB. This of course is only a rough sketch, and it would be possible to improve on many things. But it has this virtue that it is, with its wealth of material and apparent antitheses, dramatically very homogenous and tight. The difficulty presented by the dialogue depends on the bringing into relief the various deviations within the psychological makeup of the Emperor in relation to the Young Man. Some analogies with *The Bacchae* by Euripides have been made with deliberate intent and cannot be regarded as plagiarism. I am far from thrusting anything upon you and limiting your freedom, and perhaps you will discover a better dramatic solution to the fundamental problem under consideration. But I reckon that the solution I am suggesting to you is very successful, thanks to its dramatic continuity and accumulation of scenic activity, which at any rate ought to be the point in the theatre. I should be terribly pleased to hear what you think of this, and I should like to have news from you about it as quickly as possible. I instinctively fear you will object to being constrained by someone else's idea. But I think that the idea as such ought not to be alien to you, for I took away the impression of our conversations together on a subject we approached along parallel lines. I am chiefly concerned only with the external dramatic crux in which it was essential to involve the central characters – while the fundamental inner motives remain completely the same.

You won't be offended by the orgiastic action? I reckon it is inevitable in bringing into relief the fundamental motives of the drama. My favourite idea (about the secret relationship between Christ and Dionysus) will certainly be familiar to you as well. With regard to the external scenic aspect, it is difficult to dream of more – and that is precisely what so attracts me. At any rate, my friend, think carefully about this, and write to me in detail what you think of this. I do not hide from you that the question of this drama is to some extent the question of my further artistic existence – so deeply has this idea struck a root within my inner being. In view of this, I almost have the face to order you to work on it! I am afraid that you will be offended by the total lack of intimacy and the glaring, heated passion of this colouristically blinding idea, but I reckon that these are conditions *sine qua non* of the theatre.[14]

At this juncture, work on *King Roger* broke off. Iwaszkiewicz made his way to Warsaw following the reconstitution of the Polish state, leaving the composer trapped in the Ukraine for a further year. Until such a time as progress could be made on the libretto, Szymanowski occupied himself almost exclusively on his novel, *Efebos*. Here he expanded upon and clarified matters relating to the subject and ideology of the projected opera.[15]

Given the circumstances in which he found himself while writing *Efebos*, it is perhaps not so strange that Szymanowski should hide away in his private artistic world. It is even more surprising to find him continuing to inhabit this world for so long after his arrival in independent Poland at the end of 1919. His co-librettist, Iwaszkiewicz, who in any case had never been particularly enthusiastic about the Sicilian project, found the whole idea of an opera based on a medieval subject entirely irrelevant once he had arrived in Warsaw. On 14 September 1919 he wrote to the composer of his budding literary career in the new Poland and of the fresh circles in which he was moving:

I've published *Oktostychy*, which however has not enjoyed much success; in addition *Gody jesienne* ['Autumn Wedding'], *Demeter* (with a dedication to you), and the *Legend of St Balbin* were published in 'Zdrój' ['Spring' – an expressionist fortnightly published in Poznań], and the *Legend of the Tower of St Basil* in 'Pro arte', a new Warsaw paper. Besides this I am the representative (almost a deputy editor) of 'Zdrój' in Warsaw, and I deal with its administrative and editorial affairs in the hours I have free from my position as private tutor at Prince Woroniecki's – you must have known them in Warsaw. But for me the most important thing is my friendly dealings with a whole series of young, indescribably distinguished and talented, and at the same time, beloved poets, such as Tuwim, Wierzyński, Horzyca, Lechoń, Sonimski – what is more Mietek and I (Mietek is presently going under the name of Jerzy Rytard) are forming a significant group, indeed more of a

---

[14] *Ibid.*, pp. 562–67.
[15] These aspects are examined below: *cf.* pp. 63–91.

whole literary movement possessed of strength and value. Our physiognomy is clearly defined: joy, assertion of life, the desire to infuse art into life and life into art etc. Some, like Wierzyński, are indescribably fresh, strong talents.[16]

He admitted that, although he had not given up the intention of working on the opera, he had done nothing more in the meantime. He pointedly suggested to Szymanowski that in the absence of any contribution from himself, he might perhaps write the whole thing himself: 'That would perhaps be best'.[17]

But Szymanowski was not to be deflected as he still regarded the opera as central to his very survival as an artist. At his insistence Iwaszkiewicz produced a working libretto, dated 8 June 1920. Entitled *Pasterz* ('The Shepherd'), it was little more than a versification of Szymanowski's scenario, now centred on the character of Roger II rather than Frederick. This version survives in fragmentary form with additional remarks inserted by Szymanowski.[18] The material for Act I is not significantly different from that of the final version. There are only minor changes of text and word-order, although a large 'hair-pin' *crescendo* sign on p. 10 signifies the requirement to expand Roksana's response to the Shepherd's song, and in the left-hand margin at the start of the shepherd's aria, 'Mój Bóg jest piękny' ('My God is beautiful'), there is a note in Szymanowski's hand: 'A dur' [A Major] and the musical incipit of the aria, albeit without the 'Lydian' raised fourth (D sharp) which perhaps was linked in the composer's mind with Bassareus, as Dionysus was known in Lydia and Thrace.

The entire second act is missing, and the sketchy remains of the third, set in the ruins of the theatre at Syracuse, correspond to Szymanowski's original scheme, namely a Bacchanalia followed by Roger's surrender to Dionysus. For the first time, Roger's consort, Roksana, is named.

> You hear? –
> And only the quiet song of the flute
> Sounded on this side

---

[16] *Ibid.*, p. 583. The writers mentioned were all associated with the periodical *Skamander*, published from 1920 onwards. Skamander, the river on which Troy stood, was a symbol of regeneration in Wyspiański's drama *Acropolis*, and the manifesto of the group emphasised the importance of a re-adjustment to the post-war political situation and with it a desire to immerse themselves in the present as opposed to the realms of so-called beautiful illusion. Of the authors mentioned, Szymanowski himself had links with Julian Tuwim (1894–1953), whose texts he used in the song-cycle *Słopiewnie*; Jerzy Rytard (1899–1970), who provided him with the first version of the libretto for the ballet *Harnasie*, and Jan Lechoń (1899–1956) who assisted him at the time of the Paris production of *Harnasie* in 1936.

[17] *Ibid.*, p. 584.

[18] It is housed in the Polish Composers' Archive in the Warsaw University Library (Mus. CXXV rps 8).

[crossed out: 'Where did he go?'] Roger, you here? [crossed out: 'flute']

Roger: But I want to find him.

Rok[sana]: Renounce thoughts of ignoring trial...
[crossed out: 'Now I am yours
He is not taking [me]
He is not appearing to me now
He will not guide me now
In the woods and forests'.]
He went off... into the distance he returned to the mountains
On the fruit-pulp of emerald pathways
There his golden steps go
Between the sharp edges of stones
Over the sharp edges of stones.
He buries his feet [crossed out: 'he washes his blood-stained']
In waves of torrents of wild mountains
And the good water kisses them
With thousands of good, cold lips

Roger: I must see the Shepherd

Rok: (enticingly) My lips are sweet,
Warm them with kisses
[Crossed out: 'Say'] Lead me to your bedroom
My servants will make
A fragrant bed for us.
I will inflame your [crossed out: 'chilled'] weary body –

Roger: Where is the shepherd – the shepherd, the shepherd, where?

Rok: [crossed out: 'You want to see him? without fail?']
You want to see the shepherd?
So call him, let him come,   let him come!

Rog: (joyfully) How am I to call him?
How am I to summon him?
[crossed out: 'will he come?']

Rok: Call: Evoe! Bacchus! Evoe!

Roger: (he recoils terrorstruck)

Rok: The mysterious distant call!
The mysterious song!
The Song of Life!
Call him; ah, call!
In the light of the rays of the sun
he will come!
Do you hear the sound of the flute?

Rok: Evoe! Bacchus! Evoe!
(Silence. In the distance flutes [crossed out: 'of Pan'] sound. In the bushes, in the thickets together with the rising sun some sort of

concealed life stirs. Rustling. Breezes. Imperceptible awakening
of the elemental forces of Nature. Flutes are heard (calls).)

Roger:	Come, shepherd, come!
Distant chorus:	Evoe!
	Come to us
	Bright one!
	[crossed out: 'you, O shining one!']
	The sheen of leopard skin
	The juice of grape-bunches
	And give
	intoxication
	Evoe!
Rok:	He comes, he comes!
	(She throws her grey cloak from her shoulders. She appears in the guise of a maenad [crossed out: 'Roger recoils terrified into Edrisi's embrace']
Rok:	Ho! ho! Bacchus! Ho! ho!
	(she shakes a thyrsis)
Rok:	You called him, Roger.
	You yourself wanted him to
	appear for the third time
	You summoned him
	now for the third time
	He will come, now, he will come!
	Now he comes, he comes now!
	(She shakes a thyrsis [crossed out: 'she runs'] she vanishes amongst blocks of marble [Szymanowski's insertion: 'after a moment she appears higher up on the steps of the theatre'], where maenads, satyrs, beautiful youths come increasingly into view. Roger clasps Edrisi.)
Roger:	O tell me, [Crossed out: 'poet'] Edrisi,
	[crossed out: 'Tell me friend']
	What means this
	bright dream?
	It wakens in my heart
	[crossed out: 'cool'] Feverish, lively fear
	I want [crossed out: 'under his feet']
	to place under his feet
	the kingly scarlet robe
	Who is this magical shepherd
	Whence comes this fear in my heart?
Edrisi:	From your anxiety
	is born divine existence

Rok:	Do you hear how your heart
	dies in delight – Hush?
Roger:	Do you hear how like leaves
	One whisper penetrates
	And drops sway to and fro?
	Like tears of joy?
	Do you hear how like an echo
	they murmur the joyous song –
	When he rises together with the sun
	He will come to us.
Choir:	You hear the sound of the flute?
	Pan plays!
	Together with the sun he rises
	And will come to us.
	Evoe! Bacchus! Evoe!
	Ho, ho! Bacchus! Ho, ho!
	[crossed out: 'Edrisi']: the magic of the sun's powers
Choir:	Ho, ho! Bacchus! Ho, ho!
Edrisi:	Humble yourself before him, King.
Rok:	Ho ho, Bacchus, ho ho!
	and [crossed out: 'reveal the darkness']
Roger:	Reveal the darkness of the soul
	ho ho, Bacchus, ho ho!
	Fall at his feet!
	ho ho, Bacchus, ho ho!
	Breathe sweet bliss on you

With supra-sunny lips

You envelop the soul

Lurk in the most secretive beings

You give him your life

And he gives you His

As Iwaszkiewicz later admitted, his original version of the last act was far simpler than that eventually substituted by Szymanowski himself:

Roger not only discovered Dionysus in the ruins of the old theatre, but followed him and what is more flung himself into the chaos of the mysterious Dionysian cult, leaving Edrisi and Roksana on stage. It was contrary to history, but dramatically more logical. Roger not only recognised Dionysus in the shepherd, but followed him into the darkness, abandoning everything for him. Szymanowski changed this conclusion. Perhaps he did not understand that ultimate repudiation of the world I had introduced; perhaps he considered my simple conclusion to be a superfluous elucidation. Whatever the reason, he cast my third act aside, and substituted the almost completely different one that today appears in the opera, and which even has a different style from my part.[19]

Szymanowski was reasonably content with the earlier parts of the libretto and immediately started work on musical composition. The first act, composed at the house of his friend Stefan Spiess, came to him relatively easily, but although he had described the libretto as marvellous in a letter to his publisher, Emil Hertzka,[20] reservations soon began to surface. On 11 September 1920, he wrote to Iwaszkiewicz, at that time away from Warsaw on military service, that his basic mood was one of bad temper and irritation

> chiefly because, thanks to continual meetings and other similar such idiocies, I am unable to work on *The Shepherd* as I should like. I am continually torn away from it on the most stupid matters. I have written the beginning of the second act (up to the entry of the Shepherd) – but what sort of work can I do on ten minutes a day. And I should so like you to be here, as I think certain small changes would be desirable there – not to the words, but the situation – and I should not like to make these without you. It is to do with the fact that *the moment of the dance* must be more categorically and logically prepared. In other words the Shepherd and the others must have sufficient reason for ceasing to sing in favour of the dance.[21]

Almost a month later, on 5 October, he informed Iwaszkiewicz that he had unilaterally introduced the necessary revisions so as to throw the dance element into sharp relief:

> I wanted to send all this to you for your *approbatura* – but simply did not have the time, so I decided on making a poetic revision with you post factum – which we can always do. I should definitely have finished the whole thing, or at least the second act, had I not been interrupted so much – to the extent that I've stopped in the middle – and because of my expedition work is again postponed *ad calendas graecas* – which is an indescribable irritation for me.[22]

[19] Iwaskiewicz, *op. cit.*, p. 80.
[20] Letter dated 23 June 1920, in Teresa Chylińska (ed.), *Karol Szymanowski Korespondencja*, Tom 2, 1920–1926, Polskie Wydawnictwo Muzyczne, Kraków 1994, p. 113.
[21] *Ibid.*, p. 141.
[22] *Ibid.*, p. 152.

The 'expedition' to which Szymanowski referred was a cultural mission to Paris and London, undertaken in the final months of 1920 with the critic and former librarian to the Imperial court in Vienna, Hans Effenberg-Śliwiński (1884–1950). At the urging of his friends, the violinist Paweł Kochański and pianist Artur Rubinstein, he resigned from this project in order to visit the USA early in 1921 in the hope of furthering his career. His American diary reveals that it was there, on 4 February 1921, that he properly settled down to revise the libretto. By 11 February, the vital changes had been made to the third act, but it was not until 20 March, after he had returned from a trip to Florida and Cuba, that Szymanowski wrote to Iwaszkiewcz to describe the extent of the revision:

> My work consisted of the following things: I wrote the scenic details (and notes for the director) to all the acts. In the first and second acts I changed some phrases, and added a longer 'solo' for Roksana in the first act and for Roger in the second, where in the end they 'sing' too little and too irregularly (at any rate the additions are dramatically justifiable). On the other hand I have fundamentally changed the third act. Don't you think that its symbolism was too glaring and what is worse – too naive (as an idea). I have preferred to bury everything in darkness and night, to conceal the shepherd and his surroundings – so that the spectator himself ought to surmise what it is about, or else if he is a dolt, leave the theatre baffled, which I wish on him from the depths of my heart. On the other hand I have brought Roksana to the fore, and still more the king who is the real hero of this act. Of course this act is markedly worse poetically than the others, but do you concede that the basis is apt?[23]

Iwaszkiewicz was not over-enthusiastic about these changes, informing Szymanowski that his remodelling of the third act definitely did not appeal to him,

> but it is your work and you have a complete right to do what you like with it, and besides you are right that in texture it was as yet too transparent and naive, although hugely expressive.[24]

Much later, Iwaszkiewicz admitted that the underlying problem of their entire collaboration lay in the fact that each of them saw something different in *King Roger*, and he persisted to the end in his view that Szymanowski's transformation of Act III was not an improvement:

> Szymanowski wanted to express in this opera things which I did not very well comprehend and so I rather unwillingly worked on the libretto. Szymanowski

---

[23] *Ibid.*, pp. 217–18.
[24] *Ibid.*, p. 233. Undated letter, but sent from Warsaw in mid-April 1921.

sensed this – he introduced alterations which not only did not change the content for the better, but weakened the drama.[25]

There is little doubt that Szymanowski experimented with a musical setting even before the libretto was written. Serge Puzenkin, a music-teacher in Elizavetgrad, recalled that, as early as 1919, Szymanowski 'often played fragments from the opera he was writing during those years'.[26] But since he was waiting for Iwaszkiewicz to produce a libretto, it was only in September 1920 in Warsaw that he began serious work on the sketch. By February 1921, while staying in New York, he had finished Acts I and II in short score, and in July 1921, after his return to Poland, he managed to complete the final act. The scoring was to take a further three years, and indeed became something of a chore as he became pre-occupied with the development of a radically different creative approach based on Polish highland music. In October 1922 he wrote of his frustration to Kochański, stating that he was continually sitting up to his ears in the opera, and that as long as he was unable to complete it, he could not begin anything new. At that time, he estimated it would take a further three or four months. In the event, he was faced with so many distractions that it took almost another year to complete the second act:

> I have just today completed the second act of Roger – the third still remains – a little shorter. I had a detailed look through it today and I must admit – with a certain *pride*. It is perhaps my best thing – in any case, the *deepest* in conception. This pleases me a little, because in general I have gone through some boredom on its account. Incidentally I dream of something new.[27]

This letter to Kochański was written from Gierkany, an estate belonging to Thomas Zan, a banker and agrarian, where Szymanowski stayed for two months. It was again thanks to Zan's hospitality that the composer was at last able to complete the final act the following year. It had proved to be an increasingly heavy burden, even though by January 1924 only a small portion remained to be completed:

> the strange thing is that at present only some ten pages of the score of the *Shepherd* are missing – but I do not feel I literally have the strength to finish it. This is simply a scandal, because I have already sent off the first act to be printed.[28]

---

[25] *Op. cit.*, p. 79.

[26] Quoted in Chylińska, *Karol Szymanowski i jego epoka*, Vol. 1, *op. cit.*, p. 539.

[27] Letter to Paweł Kochański dated 18 August 1923, in *Karol Szymanowski Korespondencja*, Vol. 2, *op. cit.*, I, p. 624.

[28] *Ibid.*, I, p. 720.

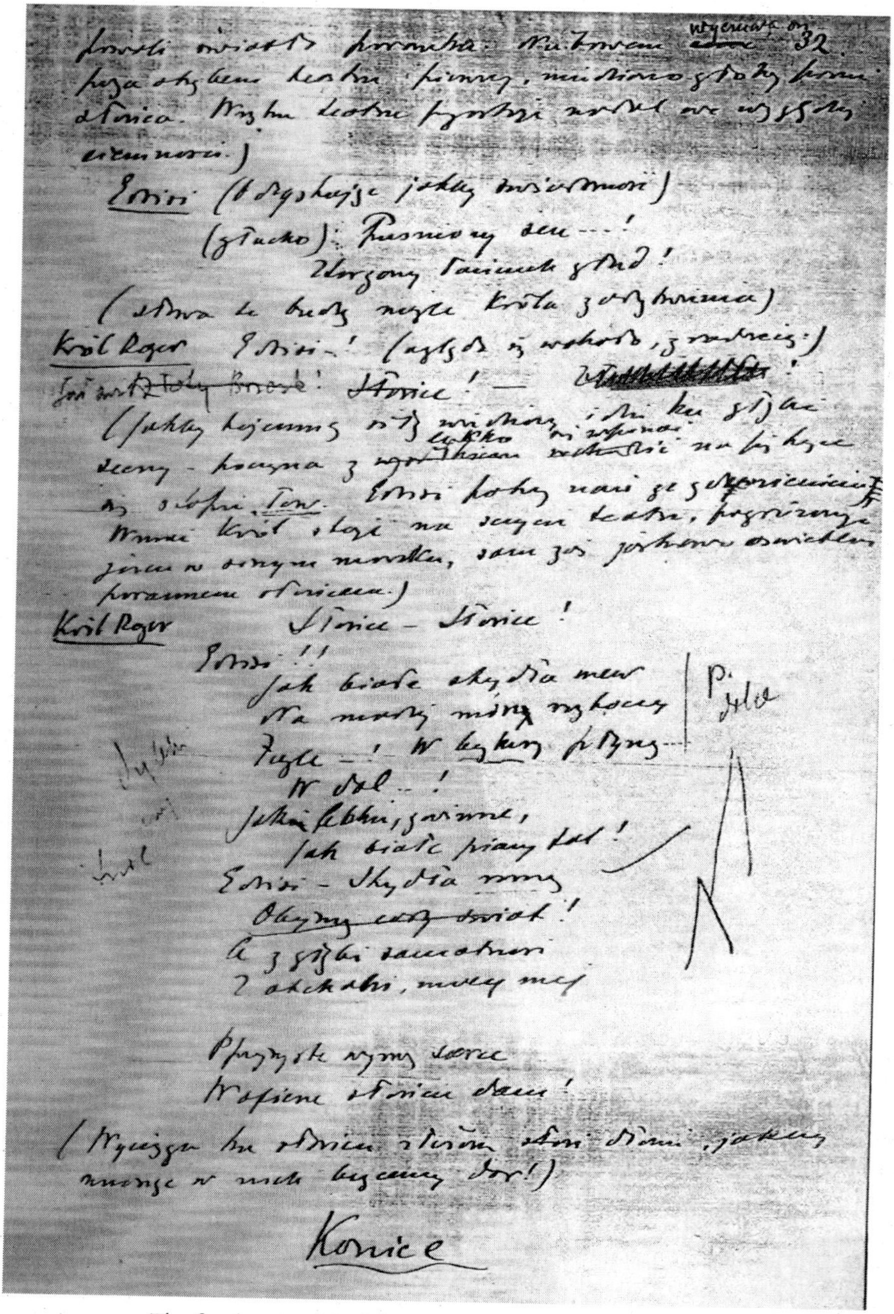

The final page of the libretto as revised by Szymanowski

Dorothy Jordan Robinson, the dedicatee of King Roger, *and her daughter*

Szymanowski still seemed unable, or unwilling, to have done with the project the following March:

> Concerning my work, I wrote 6 mazurkas in Zakopane and ... did not finish *Roger* which has got stuck like a bone in the throat![29]

On 12 August, by contrast, he was able to report success:

> And here today – hurrah! – I have at last finished *Roger*. I have a certain sense of liberation, and at the same time a certain sadness. I am terribly tired, because that bit in the third act which remained to be done is a real instrumental-contrapuntal hocus-pocus, so unfortunately I am not sure that I have extricated myself from it with honour![30]

It is perhaps not surprising that in the end Szymanowski experienced such difficulty in leaving the work behind him. In some ways it marked a final farewell to the 'Mediterranean' phase of his artistic career, built on a love of the cultures of antiquity, made all the more poignant as 'that bit in the

---

[29] *Ibid.*, II, p. 67.
[30] *Ibid.*, II, pp. 150–51.

third act', as will become evident, was the well-nigh irresistible summons of Dionysus to the hedonistic life.

King Roger was dedicated to Dorothy Jordan Robinson (1885–1976), with whom Szymanowski had first become acquainted during his stay in America in 1921. Descended from an old Boston family – her father, Eben Dyer Jordan, had provided funds for the New England Conservatory in Boston as well as the Boston Opera – she supported Szymanowski financially for a number of years in the late 1920s and early '30s. He presented her with the earliest sketches for the opera, which are now lodged in the Library of Congress, Washington.

IV
The Ideology
of *King Roger*

It would not be an exaggeration to claim that the whole of Szymanowski's life-experience contributed to the fashioning of *King Roger*. As shall be seen, the ideology of the work was clearly based on his knowledge of the culture of antiquity and a personal philosophy based around his readings of Pater, Nietzsche, Merezhkovsky and Miciński, among others. On the other hand, its geographical setting and historical background inevitably drew directly on memories of his travels. Of course, *King Roger* is not unique in drawing on mediaeval Sicily as a backdrop for an opera: so, too, did Rossini's *Tancredi* (1813), Bellini's *I pirata* (1827), Meyerbeer's *Robert le diable* (1831) and Verdi's *Les vêpres siciliennes* (1855). What is different here is the care and attention Szymanowski lavished on ensuring the authenticity of the setting – an aspect of the work all too often ignored, alas, in recent reductive productions.[1]

Szymanowski had long been a devotee of Italy and her art, as he emphasised in a letter to Zdzisław Jachimecki in 1910:

> If Italy did not exist, then I also could not exist. I am not a painter or sculptor, but when I walk through the museums, the churches and finally the streets, when I look on those elevated noble works, eternally smiling down serenely and tolerantly on all base, soulless bunglers – when I become aware of those entire generations of the most beautiful, the most talented people, then I feel it is worth living and working [...].[2]

In *King Roger* he was able to express his affection for the Sicily he had visited in 1911 and 1914, on both occasions in the company of Stefan Spiess, whose memoir provides invaluable information on their travels together. He remembered that Szymanowski was not given to systematic, pedantic studies of works of art but nonetheless always sensed the heart of the matter, detailing:

> his totally unique absorption in impressions, his inquisitiveness and his knack of forming – with the help of a rich imagination and co-ordination of

¹ *Cf.* pp. 151–55, below.
² Letter dated 4 December 1910, in *Karol Szymanowski Korespondencja*, Vol. 1, *op. cit.*, p. 245.

Szymanowski in the ruins of the amphitheatre at Taormina in 1911

impressions with knowledge previously acquired – a full historical picture of the country being visited.[3]

Their first tour together started in Florence, after which they travelled to Rome and then through Calabria to Sicily, eventually arriving in Palermo, where they stayed at the Villa Igiea Grand Hotel. Szymanowski informed Fitelberg that

> the day after tomorrow (2nd [May]) we leave here and tour Sicily (Girgenti, Syracuse, Taormina), then by ship to Naples.[4]

Szymanowski described himself as being in a constant state of rapture. Spiess provided details of some of their experiences in his memoir:

> We made an excursion to Segesta, beautifully situated amidst hillocks, lost, lonely in the depths of a valley. After we had been going along this valley for such a long time that it now seemed monotonous to us, we suddenly saw emerging from behind the curves of a hill a pale yellow temple with Doric columns, as if brought live from Greece.[5]

They also visited the amphitheatre at Syracuse which Szymanowski drew on for the setting of the final act of *King Roger*, and of course

> the palace chapel with the tombs of Roger and his descendants in the Cathedral in Palermo together with the splendid Romanesque church in Monreale [...] had an influence on the scenario for Act I.[6]

As Szymanowski's aim was the reconciliation of apparently exclusive traditions and the effecting of a grand humanist synthesis, it is not surprising that he should have found the Sicily of Roger II such an appealing setting for the opera. Roger (1095–1154), the most important of the Sicilian Norman kings, succeeded in building up the third-largest kingdom in the Europe of the time and establishing a court, the magnificence of which eclipsed those of England, France and the Holy Roman Empire. The meteoric rise of the Normans in southern Italy dated from 1016 when they came to the aid of the exiled Lombard, Melus of Bari, and never left. In the following decades they were at various times pitted against the Holy Roman Empire, the papacy, the Byzantine Empire which still controlled Apulia and Calabria, and Saracen forces using Sicily as a base for their attacks throughout the region. The key figures behind this southern Norman Conquest were Robert and Roger de Hautville, sons of Tancred de Hautville who virtually

---

[3] Stefan Spiess, 'Ze wspomnień melomana' ('From the Memoirs of a Melomane') (1963), in *Karol Szymanowski we wspomnieniach*, *op. cit.*, pp. 59–60.

[4] Letter dated 30 April 1911, in Chylińska (ed.), *op. cit.*, p. 263.

[5] *Loc. cit.*, p. 58.

[6] *Ibid.*, p. 60.

threw them out of Normandy to make their fortunes further afield. Robert (d. 1085) established himself as Duke of Apulia and Roger I (d. 1101) as Great Count of Sicily. Roger II, his third and only surviving son, consolidated his position as absolute monarch of both regions only with some difficulty. He was recognised as Duke of Apulia, Calabria and Sicily in 1128 by Pope Honorius, but it was only after supporting the claims of Anacletus for the papacy in 1130 that he was formally granted the crown of Sicily, Calabria and Apulia, the principality of Capua, the 'honour of Naples' and the assistance of the papal city of Benevento in time of war.

Roger's reign, though sustained of necessity by merciless responses to attempts to undermine his authority, was characterised by a unique cosmopolitanism. Residing in Palermo, which at that time had a population of some 300,000,[7] Roger ruled over a diverse population of native Sicilians, Norman settlers, and the remnants of earlier invasions and occupations of the island – notably Roman, Greek and Arab. All ethnic groups were tolerated, and the years of peace and relative stability during Roger's reign saw a flowering of an utterly unique culture in which seemingly incompatible elements were fused together. One such example is the Cappella Palatina on the first floor of Roger's palace in Palermo. It was started in 1129 and eventually consecrated on Palm Sunday 1140. Its western-styled nave was combined with pointed arches in Arab style and a cupola with a Byzantine mosaic of Christ Pantocrator gazing out in benediction. Mosaics elsewhere in the building carry both Greek and Latin inscriptions, while the Arab-styled, honey-combed ceiling is decorated with figures from Persian and Indian legend. This building is of particular interest since Szymanowski evidently used it in his description of the set for the first act of the opera.

Roger himself led a life in which he contrived to combine the roles of both Christian prince and sultan. He drew on Byzantine concepts of monarchy:

> a mystically-tinged absolutism in which the monarch, as God's viceroy, lived remote and elevated from his subjects, in a magnificence that reflected his intermediate position between earth and heaven.[8]

His preference for Byzantine ceremonial and his reserving the right to choose his own bishops protected his independence from Rome. At the same time, he was clearly at home in the Saracen world and was even described as being oriental in appearance. His palace housed a harem for women and eunuchs, and his kitchens were supervised by Arab cooks. He spoke both Greek and Arabic, and the strong Saracen influence was evident in the pursuit of

---

[7] By comparison, London at the time had 30,000 inhabitants.
[8] John Julius Norwich, *The Normans in Sicily*, Penguin Books, Harmondsworth, 1967, pp. 433–44.

The Cappella Palatina in Palermo

scientific enquiry.[9] He himself was especially interested in astronomy and astrology, and he supported Al'Idrisi[10] (who appears in Szymanowski's opera as the sage Edrisi) in the making of a silver planisphere and the compilation of a geographical volume, Al-Kitāb al-Rujāri ('The Book of King Roger'), completed in the year of Roger's death. The highest, though undoubtedly hyperbolic tribute to Roger, is paid in the dedication of this text:

> the best and most celebrated of monarchs. He unites high intellect and goodness; to these are joined his resolution, sharp understanding, deep spirit, foresight, his skill in all measures, which betray a masterful intellect [...]. His sleep is as the awakening of other men. I cannot enumerate his knowledge of the exact and technical sciences, nor set bounds to his wisdom.[11]

It is the tension between Norman-Byzantine kingship and the alternative civilisations of the Mediterranean that is the background to the opera. The

[9] The Roman Church had for centuries before and after this period discouraged secular studies, meaning that the leading scholars in the fields of mathematics, astronomy and the natural sciences were Muslim. It was also largely thanks to them that many Greek and Latin works from classical civilisation were preserved only in Arabic translation following their destruction during the Dark Ages.

[10] Abu Abdullah Mohammed al-Edrisi (or Idrisi) was born c. 1100 in Sabtah, Morocco, and died there or in Sicily c. 1165 or 1166. He entered the service of Roger II around 1145, and while at Palermo produced a major geographical study ('The Pleasure Excursion of One who is Eager to Traverse the Regions of the World').

[11] Quoted in Richard F. Cassady, *The Norman Achievement*, Guild Publishing, London, 1987, p. 231.

tension exists within Roger himself, and the conflict of ideas and clashes of culture that develop are endowed with an ever-deepening significance, for Szymanowski's opera is the record of a spiritual or psychological odyssey, at the close of which the king has recognised and integrated the apparently conflicting life-forces within his own being. As the work proceeds, Szymanowski has recourse to increasingly powerful, primordial cultural symbols, the stark simplicity of the stage action being stripped of all inessentials.

The action of the opera, in spite of the appearance of two historical figures and the authenticity of the setting, is a fiction. As noted in the preceding chapter, it takes as its starting point a reworking of Euripides' *The Bacchae*,[12] leading to a manifestation of Dionysus, the symbol of an ecstasy that cannot be explained away by reason or rationality. As the god of wine and of joy in nature, Dionysus offers release from the tensions of civilised life. In both *The Bacchae* and *King Roger*, the central characters attempt to exert their authority in face of the Dionysian challenge. In Euripides' play Pentheus, King of Phebes, unsuccessfully attempts to bind the messenger of the God, and is ultimately torn to shreds by Maenads led by his own mother. It has been observed that Pentheus is in reality Dionysiac by nature and, when opposed, 'his instinctive recourse is to the same kind of "berserk" behaviour which he is proposing to check and punish.'[13] He wears a puritanical mask, which Dionysus is easily able to shatter before making the king his sacrificial victim. In contrast, Roger, though troubled and profoundly disturbed by the Shepherd, abandons force and acknowledges and conquers the Dionysian within himself, thus avoiding the savage end which met Pentheus.

Further fascinating light is thrown upon the entire Sicilian project by a reading of what remains of Szymanowski's novel, *Efebos* ('The Youth'). The novel was in some ways a form of creative theorising which dealt with subjects closely connected with the ideology of *King Roger*, ranging from superficial considerations of stagecraft to more profound philosophical, erotic and aesthetic matters. In all probability, Szymanowski would not have taken up this literary project had he found himself in happier circumstances. The outbreak of the Bolshevik Revolution in October 1917 forced the family to flee their country estate for a town house in Elizavetgrad, thereby abandoning Tymoszówka to what the composer himself described as

[12] *Cf.* p. 42, above.
[13] Philip Vellacott, 'Introduction' in Euripides, *The Bacchae and Other Plays*, trans. Philip Vellacott, Penguin, Harmondsworth, 1954, p. 31.

'a novel concept of "agrarian reform", taking in not only the land but also the shirts, furniture and, above all, the cellars of the previous owners!'[14]

Caught up in the civil war which ensued, Szymanowski spent whole nights at a time patrolling 'with rifle and revolver, encountering everything which before would have made me faint at the very least – corpses, the wounded, terrible bands of robbers, etc.'[15] Under such horrific circumstances, he found himself unable to compose and by January 1918 was 'writing a little – without any pretensions of course – but simply to get some things off my chest'.[16] By the end of 1918, he believed that the time he had spent in Elizavetgrad had finished him for good artistically, but to justify his musical 'sterilité', he had 'banged out the first, huge volume of a novel and got down to the second', and in the same letter, he warned the Kochańskis not to smile at his pretensions to authorship, as it really was a 'very interesting novel!'[17]

Unfortunately, only fragments of *Efebos* survive. Although Szymanowski believed that it was worthy of publication – at least in part – he was unwilling to sanction its release during the lifetime of his mother because of its explicitly homosexual content. In fact, *Efebos* was something of an 'apologia pro suae vitae' and, in the composer's words, explored the question of love deeply, 'rendering any further commentary superfluous'.[18] The manuscript was bequeathed to Iwaszkiewicz for safe-keeping, and was almost totally destroyed during the first Nazi raids on Warsaw in 1939. The surviving materials consist of the following:

1) detailed plan (not, however, of the final version);
2) title pages and dedication;
3) Introduction;
4) fragmentary materials for chapters IV, V and IX;
5) 'Symposium' (not in its original form, but based on a Russian translation made by Szymanowski for Borys Kochno and rediscovered by Teresa Chylińska in Paris in 1981);
6) 'The Tale of the Miracle of the Saintly Youth Enoch Porfiry, Iconographer' (partially preserved);
7) annex and scraps (loose, unconnected materials of an aphoristic nature meant for inclusion in *Efebos*);
8) various short passages devoted to a number of different topics, almost certainly intended for inclusion in *Efebos*;

---

[14] Letter to Ludwik Uniechowski, dated 29 November 1917 in Chylińska (ed.), *Karol Szymanowski Korespondencja, op. cit.*, Vol. 1, p. 517.
[15] Letter to Zdzisław Jachimecki, written before 27 June 1918, in *ibid.*, p. 531.
[16] Letter to Jarosław Iwaszkiewicz, dated 16 January 1918, in *ibid.*, p. 523.
[17] Letter dated 15 November 1918, in *ibid.*, p. 568.
[18] *Karol Szymanowsi Pisma*, Vol. 2, *op. cit.*, p. 127.

9) early sketches and drafts of passages from the Introduction and 'Symposium'.

There is also have a useful secondary source in Iwaszkiewicz's account of the contents of *Efebos* in *Spotkania z Szymanowskim* ('Meetings with Szymanowski'), published in 1947.[19]

Like *King Roger*, *Efebos* reflected Szymanowski's profound love and knowledge of Mediterranean cultures, springing from an 'intense, majestic vision of Italy in all her imperious beauty and seductive grace'.[20] This vision of Italy originated, not surprisingly, in an attempt to escape from the grim realities of life in Elizavetgrad. Iwaszkiewicz recalled that at the time of writing Szymanowski seemed to live in a different world, surrounded by books 'which were an echo, a completion and supplement to his trips (to Italy, Sicily and Africa)'.[21] In the introduction to the novel, the composer himself acknowledged that *Efebos* was at first a piece of escapism, written

> as a sweet solace and sweet remembrance of the past, as a way of blocking off, by means of a magical vision of Italy called forth from memory, the black abyss of an unending succession of days, weeks and months spent in the most terrible external circumstances.[22]

With the passing of time, however, Italy

> appeared like a distant mirage, already dimmed by the subtle mist of the intervening years, only half emerging from the eye's forgetfulness – and the inevitable and fatal consequence of this is that everything which forms the natural background of the story, [...] appears faded and lifeless, with the muted hues of a gobelin rather than the throbbing colours of immediate experience.[23]

Notwithstanding, the inner story of the hero of *Efebos* began to emerge, proceeding step by step towards a wider understanding of life, its duties and its deep significance:

> the history of a gradual liberation from various types of traditional, inherited slavery by an increasingly clear mirage of the true freedom of the soul, springing from love and an independence, formulated not from the point of view of this or that social, religious or moral doctrine, but flowering as if by itself from the fertile soul of the human soul's deepest layers and most intimate relationship with its own life...[24]

---

[19] *Op. cit.*, pp. 85–96.
[20] *Karol Szymanowsi Pisma*, Vol. 2, *op. cit.*, p. 126.
[21] *Op. cit.*, p. 65.
[22] *Karol Szymanowsi Pisma*, Vol. 2, *op. cit.*, p. 125.
[23] *Ibid.*, p. 126.
[24] *Ibid.*, p. 126.

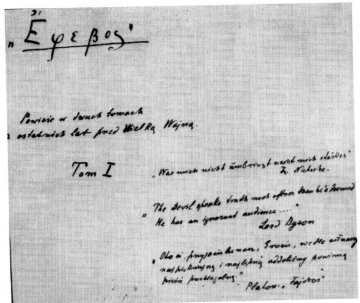

The title-page of Efebos. *The text reads:*
'Novel in two volumes set in the years immediately preceding the Great War
Volume I   'What does not kill me makes me stronger'
                                                    Fr. Nietzsche
                    'The Devil speaks truth much oftner than he's deemed
                    [But] he has an ignorant audience…'
                                                    Lord Byron
                    'And so, in propitiation to you, our friend Eros, we offer
                    the best, most beautiful song of which we are capable.'
                                                    Plato: Phaedrus

Efebos concerned the relationship between two characters. Both were Poles, reared in that

> now bygone epoch of the nation's captivity. [...] The youthful Prince Łowicki is, for his epoch, a typical representative of inner strength and deep emotion going to waste because of his external relationships... In seeking escape from slavery he finds it [...] eventually in love of the highest order [...], a love which is independent of all norms (of public opinion). [...] The composer, Marek Korab, is an analogous phenomenon, but he is set against a different psychic background and this is the creative nature through and through [...]. And so he defends his own *freedom*, the absolute *freedom* to create with fanatical determination.[25]

---

[25] *Ibid.*, pp. 127–28.

In tone *Efebos* was markedly patrician, being imbued with all the symptoms of a Nietzschean *Patos der Distanz*, according to which doctrine the development of the most elevated and farthest-reaching states of mankind was the work of an aristocratic society:

> a society that believes in the long ladder of order and rank and difference in value between man and man, [...] where the ruling caste constantly looks afar and looks down upon subjects and instruments, and just as constantly practises obedience and command, keeping down and keeping at a distance [...].[26]

From the outset, the dedication of *Efebos* makes clear that a line is to be drawn between the rabble on the one hand and those 'brooding solitary in high, impregnable towers upon the mystery of love' to whom the author offered his book, a flower 'grown on the uplands of Satanic Conceit or Angelic Humility in the face of the Hidden Blows of Fate.'[27] Furthermore, in the course of the introduction, Szymanowski focussed on the birth of two mutually exclusive forces from the ashes of shattered, post-war Europe:

> the internationalism of the proletariat masses which is destructive in the very assumptions which underlie it, and in some measure a narrow-minded and egoistic nationalism which has been intensified by the political liberation of a whole series of young, national entities, just emerging onto the historical stage.[28]

Against these two contradictory forces, Szymanowski set his own favourite daydream: 'pan-Europeanism', which he equated with 'a gathering together of the best individuals around the greatest conquests of a distinctive, spiritual culture.'[29] It is perhaps significant that this union was seen as a conspiracy of solitary men – reflected in the final, but splendid isolation of the hero of *King Roger* who, after his encounter with the forces of Dionysus, tears out his limpid heart and in solitude gives it in offering to the rising sun.

But however elevated *Efebos* undoubtedly became, it had humble enough origins as a continuation of a short story, written purely for enjoyment by one of Szymanowski's cousins, Michał Kruszyński. It was a tale of boarding-school life, and the details of the friendship-love between Prince Alo Łowicki and his older companion, the gloomy Mykita, 'were sketched with great realism, bordering on the pornographic, if not outright pornography.'[30] In

[26] Nietzsche, *Jenseits von Gut und Böse* ('Beyond Good and Evil'), transl. W. Kaufmann, Vintage, New York, 1966, p. 201.
[27] *Karol Szymanowsi Pisma*, Vol. 2, *op. cit.*, p. 124.
[28] *Ibid.*, p. 128.
[29] *Ibid.*, p. 129.
[30] Iwaszkiewicz, *op. cit.*, p. 87.

Kruszyński's tale, Mykita commits suicide when the Jesuit Fathers discover the nature of his erotic predilections. Szymanowski took over the character of Prince Łowicki, mentioning Mykita only occasionally in terms of a tragic ghost from the past. Initially *Efebos* was little more than a description of the career of Łowicki, set against a lavishly described evocation of pre-war high society. But deeper issues arose once the unfortunate Łowicki is forced to part from his fiancée under dramatic circumstances, going abroad, almost an outcast from society, in a state of profound despair and incomprehension about the very nature of his being.

In Iwaszkiewicz's words, 'good spirits watch over Alo', including Baron von Rellov, a German nobleman educated in the classical tradition of Goethe and Winckelmann, as well as a 'good, wise Frenchman in Florence' and, in Rome, a celebrated Italian professor. They initiate him into the mysteries of Italian art, and also raise a series of social, political and moral questions, 'so converting the naive, Warsaw prince into a mature man. They liberate the artist from the worldly boy'.[31]

Iwaszkiewicz remarked on the careful, detailed writing of *Efebos*, which displayed erudition and artistic sensibility, and thought that one of its best sections was the description of Florence, notably the Duomo and the graves of the Medicis. From Florence, Alo moves on to Rome where new characters are introduced, some of whom were modelled on the composer's friends, notably the Countess Lanskaya, based on Natalie Davidova whose family estates were adjacent to those of the Szymanowskis in the Ukraine. Natalie was 'a beautiful person, [...] serious, intelligent, musical and full of goodness',[32] and in the novel the Natalie-Lanskaya character plays a protective role, revealing the intrigues of the other characters and leading Alo towards a more profound understanding of artistic and human qualities which hitherto he had not realised he possessed.

It is also in Rome that the Polish composer, Marek Korab, appears. Korab is a portrait of Szymanowski as one who is at least as famous as Paderewski'.[33] At this point it became apparent, according to Iwaszkiewicz, that these two central characters represented different aspects of Szymanowski's own character:

> Łowicki is Szymanowski in his youth, uncertain, learning, not understanding himself and anxiously seeking *true* love, in the end unable to find an outlet for his individuality and searching for it in literary work; in Korab, Szymanowski painted himself as he would like to be in the future: very famous and rich,

---

[31] *Ibid.*, p. 88.
[32] *Ibid.*, p. 89.
[33] *Ibid.*, pp. 91–92.

very certain of his artistic value, surrounded by general adoration and moving with ease from one success to the next.[34]

Two scenes in the second part of the novel featured important turning-points: the first was the 'Symposium', the portion rediscovered in Paris in 1981. This exhaustive, Plato-inspired discussion of love and eroticism opened Alo's eyes to the nature of his relationship with Korab, forcing him to conclude 'that he could only exist as a man and artist in the closest association with the composer'.[35] The second scene was a description of a ball given by a Prince Primoli, although for Iwaszkiewicz, one of the most memorable parts of the novel was the account of the concert which preceded the ball at which Korab's sonata was performed. Here Szymanowski paid tribute to his most celebrated performers, Paweł Kochański and Artur Rubinstein. Szymanowski described their manner of performance with great precision, and not only the inner interpretation but even their external manner [...]. With great affection he described the performers of Korab's (for which read: his own) sonata, and this purely musical episode is distinguished by its marked sincerity as distinct from a background which is a little artificial in colour. [...] this was a real pearl in the lost novel.[36]

In the course of the ball itself, Alo and Korab hold a vital conversation during which their mutual dependency on each other becomes clear. It is at this ball, however, that the devious secretary at the Russian Embassy in Rome, Gleba Nieszczerowa, 'a beautiful young man, but full of inner evil and fundamentally corrupt',[37] intrudes, accusing Alo of being a 'vulgar consumer of bought love'.[38] Korab leaves disillusioned, and the next day the desperate Alo flees Rome for Sicily. In Iwaszkiewicz's opinion, the most beautiful part of the novel followed, revealing Szymanowski to be a totally mature psychological writer. Against the background of exquisite descriptions of Palermo, whose charm he evoked splendidly, Szymanowski expertly conducted Alo through his spiritual rebirth, his humiliation, suffering and solitude, from which is gradually born creative consciousness till at last life-saving streams of creativity suddenly overflow. [...] The spiritual processes leading from amatory suffering to the overflowing of artistic creativity [...] were all described with great artistry, demonstrating that in Szymanowski there was embedded the makings of a first-rate writer.[39]

---

[34] *Ibid.*, p. 92; emphasis in original.
[35] *Ibid.*, p. 93.
[36] *Ibid.*, pp. 93–94.
[37] *Ibid.*, p. 90.
[38] *Ibid.*, p. 94.
[39] *Ibid.*, p. 94.

As the novel moved towards its climax, Szymanowski included the (partly preserved) 'Tale of the Miracle of the Saintly Youth Enoch Porfiry, Iconographer' which purported to be an example of Alo's mature literary style. As will be seen,[40] marked resemblances to the subject-matter of *King Roger* are evident here, as well as in the final scenes of *Efebos*, set in Palermo, during which Łowicki finally divests all worldly trappings to discover the true man within himself. As in *King Roger*, the closing moments are set amongst ancient ruins – in this case those of the temple at Segesta:

> There in the moonlit, pale, Sicilian night, lost in thoughts about himself and his creative work, he suddenly meets Korab. The maturity which Łowicki has attained [...] eases their discovery and understanding of each other, and their meeting in the temple becomes the starting-point of a new harmony between the two artists, the writer and the composer.[41]

Among the many illuminating links between the novel, with its underlying drift towards synthesis and psychological integration, and the opera, 'Uczta' ('The Feast' or 'Symposium') and the surviving fragments of 'The Tale of Enoch Porfiry' are of particular significance. Superficially, the 'Symposium' contains remarks from the Korab character about theatre in general, and *The Bacchae* of Euripides in particular:

> While all those Alcestes, Andromaches and Hecubas seemed to me – *mea culpa* – to be extremely boring, [...] *The Bacchae* made a simply extraordinary impression on me! That ideal, elevated 'theatricality', alas long since lost in the helpless naturalism of the cinematographic quasi-psychology of present-day drama, is, if I may put it this way, 'theatrical' *sub specie aeternitatis*, in that it is independent of the caprice of a given historic epoch. This creative process, plumbing the very depths of life, raised above the fleeting waves of everyday existence, brings it close in the truth of its feelings to the heights of *King Œdipus* and the *Oresteia* – in spite of differences in style and general creative atmosphere. And besides this, its content is closer to us, pulsating with warm blood which is more palpable and comprehensible for us.[42]

Intriguingly, Korab even goes on to reveal that he has been thinking about the possibility of using *The Bacchae* as the basis for a music drama, but had encountered insurmountable obstacles:

> First, the tragedy in its original form is not suitable for a music drama with regard to its length and oppressive unity of time and place. One would not only have to shorten it, but make extensive revisions. And it is significant

---

[40] *Cf.* pp. 82–83, below.
[41] *Ibid.*, p. 95.
[42] *Karol Szymanowsi Pisma*, Vol. 2, *op. cit.*, p. 143.

that in all contemporary adaptations, the masterpieces of antiquity lose their original, unique fascination. Even Hofmannsthal's *Elektra!*[43]

Another difficulty was the representation of Dionysus on stage, a Dionysus who, in Korab's imagination, is very similar to the Shepherd of *King Roger*:

> That ephebe with sensual lips, clothed in coloured, patterned chifon and a coat the colour of saffron, the untanned hide of a deer thrown over his shoulders, an ephebe with long coppery ringlets both sides of his beautiful, delicate, youthful face, his deep eyes burning with the fire of an inscrutable, eternal mystery! Who could play such a youth, with a flower-bedecked thyrsis in his hand, and his head crowned with ivy and scarlet roses?! Some loathsome tenor with pink tights covering his flabby calves. No, it really is impossible – Dionysus singing 'tenor'. There is the possibility of 'travesty' – some corpulent female contralto, with knock-knees and thighs the shape of a lyre, rather like Siebel in *Faust* or Pazio in *Huguenots*. No, heaven forfend! It's simply impossible.[44]

Korab reveals that he has decided to abandon opera in favour of 'pantomime', following the example of the Russian Ballet which 'has shown us how to manage things in this field, and above all, to introduce on stage that most beautiful of all things, namely a genuine youth'.[45]

These remarks were by no means merely fictional musings on the part of Korab. In a postscript to a letter, dated 26 June 1918 (i.e., at about the time the earliest plans were drawn up for *King Roger*), Szymanowski wrote to his publisher, Emil Hertzka, the Director of Universal Edition in Vienna, that he had 'an overpowering urge to work on some stage-work (ballet rather than opera)', but could not find a suitable libretto:

> I have been thinking a lot about the essence of theatre and have come to the conclusion that it is the end for opera in the literal sense. That is why I am very interested in what Schreker (one of the very few who can say anything new in this field – Stravinsky also) has said in his new opera [*Die Gezeichneten*]![46]

The other reservations, involving the difference between illusion and the reality of loathsome tenors, pink tights and flabby calves, were of course by no means original, and may even have been suggested by Tolstoy's hilarious description of an operatic performance in *War and Peace*, which Szymanowski read 'with great delight'[47] in 1916:

[43] *Ibid.*, p. 144.
[44] *Ibid.*, pp. 144–45.
[45] *Ibid.*, p. 145.
[46] *Karol Szymanowski Korespondencja*, Vol. 1. *op. cit.*, p. 535.
[47] Letter to Stefan Spiess, dated 3 July 1916, in *ibid.*, p. 467.

*A bas-relief of Dionsysus
from Herculaneum*

In the middle of the stage sat some girls in red bodices and white petticoats. One extremely fat girl in a white silk dress was sitting apart on a low bench, to the back of which a piece of green cardboard was glued. They were all singing something. When they had finished their chorus the girl in white advanced towards the prompter's box, and a man with stout legs encased in silk tights, a plume in his cap and a dagger at his waist, went up to her and began to sing and wave his arms about.

First the man in tights sang alone, then she sang, then they both paused while the orchestra played and the man fingered the hand of the girl in white, obviously waiting for the beat when they should start singing again. They sang a duet and everyone in the theatre began clapping and shouting, while the man and woman on the stage, who were playing a pair of lovers, began smiling, spreading out their arms and bowing.[48]

As has been seen, Szymanowski had only recently contemplated the possibility of a 'cross-dressing' scene involving a youth in another projected stage-work: a comic opera based on episodes from the memoirs of Benvenuto Cellini.[49] In comparison with this piece, the surviving text of which teeters on the brink of homo-erotic self-indulgence, *King Roger*, for all the 'ephebery' of

---

[48] Tolstoy, *War and Peace*, transl. Rosemary Edmonds, Penguin, Harmonsworth, 1957, p. 663.
[49] *Cf.* p. 31–32, above.

the scenes involving the Shepherd, operates on an altogether more elevated plane. As Iwaszkiewicz pointed out, it was intended to enable the composer to confront 'religious obsessions',[50] and though *The Bacchae* was undoubtedly the 'primary source' of the opera, opportunities for a broader religious discourse arose once the Dionysus of old was pitted, not against Pentheus in Thebes but against mediaeval Christianity in twelfth-century Sicily with its mingling of seemingly incompatible cultural elements. Further light is again thrown on this subject and its influence on matters of sexual ethics in the course of the 'Symposium', and especially in the section in which the Rellov character discusses the attrition of contradictory convictions drawn from two different sources, inimical to each other:

> Our true culture, everything which is [...] most valuable and elevated [...] is rooted somewhere close to the foot of the Acropolis, while we are indebted to the Bible for religious concepts and dogmatic problems always connected with religion. We have to thank some power, some truly diabolical force, for the fact that this terrible book [...] has now been poisoning our organism for nigh on 2,000 years.[51]

Rellov goes on to refer to the 'paradoxical phenomenon' of the interweaving of two mutually exclusive books – the Old and New Testaments – into European religious traditions, 'and the fact that the Church Fathers understood Christ in only the most superficial and shallow of ways'.[52] Korab develops the idea further, and in so doing offers a clear statement of Szymanowski's 'favourite' idea – the equation of sympathetic Greek gods, whether Dionysus or Eros, as in this case, with Christ. In Korab's view, the way to an understanding of the 'supreme one who once appeared here so as to redeem all the past sins of the world, [...] whose only love is life in all its unfathomable profundity [...] lies not in renunciation, a flight from the "truth" of reality',[53] a course of action which it transpires Korab himself had pursued in his youth as a consequence of early religious experiences. Taking as his 'text' Rellov's remark that the gods permit everything to those who love, Korab reflects on attaining true knowledge of what one should love in life. He recalls his first impressions of the Christ he had tried to love and serve – impressions based on the sight of the huge wooden crucifix hanging in St Mary's Church, Kraków:

> Under the high vault [...] there hangs a crucifix [...] and on it a Christ of supernatural grandeur, looking as if he had only just died in terrible agony,

[50] *Op. cit.*, p. 68.
[51] *Karol Szymanowsi Pisma*, Vol. 2, *op. cit.*, p. 158.
[52] *Ibid.*, p. 160.
[53] *Ibid.*, p. 166.

Detail of crucifix from the church of St Mary, Kraków

so marvellous and suffering a face he had. He ordered me to go into retreat and love God above all, and my neighbour as myself. I did not know what I should do, and in despair thought I was condemned to eternal torment from the Devil. For at that time I always pictured my 'neighbour' as some alien, anonymous man in grey, and how could I possibly love him? Neither did I know what to make of 'God' – I was always told he was a 'spirit' and I was unable to find a place for him in my tiny childish heart. So I could only love the crucified Christ who died in agony to redeem me from my onerous sins, and who turned his suffering face towards me from the unscalable heights of the vault. There was only one thing I did not understand: why it was that this very figure, so poor and tender, so dear and beloved, required what appeared to be impossible from everyone. And this love, and that astonishment always lingered with me until that terrifying moment when, many years later, when I was in Italy, I really saw His Face for the first time in the Brera,[54] a true likeness gazing sadly at me from the miserable remains of oil-paints on a cracked wall, devoured by moisture and the ravages of time: His real, youthful Face, which supposedly came to Leonardo in a prophetic dream! It resonated so very much more than the others, this one true likeness of Christ [...]. It was only then, looking with a tremor of the heart at Leonardo da Vinci's embodiment

[54] A district in the centre of Milan where the main art galleries are situated as well as the church and Dominican convent of Santa Maria delle Grazie, where Leonardo's *The Last Supper* may be found.

of superhuman, boundless suffering, that I suddenly felt that no-one had understood him! I realised that his word had been expounded slavishly and falsely amongst that so very intimate, narrow circle of disciples and believers – those simple, uncouth, naive people. Only then did I grasp who he really was! He – Christ – Eros!

'Before the cock shall crow thrice' – what a terrible certainty of his own isolation! After appearing for the last time at that saddest feast in the world, He, the son of God, Christ-Eros, suddenly realised that he was an alien here and that he would be handed over to the rabble! This was suffering at its deepest, the suffering of one who loved God – not Jehovah, not the menacing Adonai, the implacable judge of his followers – but of one who loved love, born in boundless freedom, in an insatiable, deep desire for Eternity.

He loved his neighbour with the mysterious, burning ardour of existence, the insatiable desire to associate with the eternal, creative essence of the world which shone with an unearthly light in the inscrutable eyes of the Lydian God with copper hair, crowned with ivy and roses, a thyrsis entwined with flowers in his hand....[55]

Emerging again here is Szymanowski's 'favourite' idea of a fusion of the old and new religions, but it was not in itself an original conception. He had long been familiar with the works of the Russian writer Dmitry Sergeyevich Merezhkovsky, and in particular the novels of the trilogy *Christ and Antichrist*. The first two, *Julian the Apostate* and *The Romance of Leonardo da Vinci: The Forerunner* are of especial relevance here. *Julian the Apostate* is specifically concerned with the Roman Emperor Julian's attempts to replace the recently recognised Christian faith with earlier religions. Conflicts between the old and the new rumble on throughout the narrative, but in the course of his initiation into the Ephesian mysteries, Julian, bathed in the rays of the rising sun, is exhorted (fruitlessly) to 'make one of the truth of the Titan [Prometheus] and the truth of the Galilean', so that he shall be 'the greatest of all that are born of women on earth.'[56] In *Leonardo da Vinci*, Leonardo is portrayed as working towards a fusion of paganism and Christianity, symbolised by the links between the paintings of Bacchus and John the Baptist. In the Bacchus, the god sat long-haired and fair as a woman; his head crowned with vine-leaves, a spotted skin round his loins, a thyrsus in his hand. In Merezhkowsky's highly fanciful romance, the Bacchus was abandoned, and Leonardo worked feverishly on a new work, in which 'the face and figure of a naked youth, womanish, seductively beautiful' appears.

[55] *Karol Szymanowsi Pisma*, Vol. 2, *op. cit.*, pp. 166-7.
[56] Dmitri Merejkowski, *Julian the Apostate*, transl. Bernard Guilbert Guerney, The Modern Library, New York, 1929, p. 97.

Bacchus and St John the Baptist by Leonardo da Vinci

But instead of the leopard's skin he wore a garment of camel's hair; instead of the thyrsus he carried a cross. Smiling, with bent head, as if listening, all expectation, all curiosity, yet half afraid, he pointed with one hand to the cross...[57]

In *King Roger* the Shepherd, the young man who appears at the court of the King, clearly exhibits the traditional trappings of a votary of Dionysus, although describing his God in Christian terms as a good shepherd, roaming stony trails and mountain paths, seeking lost flocks. Notwithstanding, the shepherd is clearly a sexually subversive influence, and the nature of the religious-sexual conflict which underlies the main narratives of both *Efebos* and *King Roger* is further illuminated in some additional material associated with the novel. This material takes the form of a series of unpolished texts, jottings perhaps intended for inclusion at a later date, and in one of these texts Szymanowski makes clear his belief that religion contributed to a permanent deviation from the direct, natural line of psychic development, because of 'the correlation of 'sin' and 'the whole sphere of "love". [...] In other words, an awful, tormenting deflection of all natural instincts occurs during childhood and youth.'[58] In this respect, religious education had to be

[57] Dmitry Sergeyevich Merezhkovsky, *The Romance of Leonardo da Vinci: The Forerunner*, transl. Herbert Trench, Putnam, New York and London, 1904, pp. 441–42.
[58] *Karol Szymanowsi Pisma*, Vol. 2, *op. cit.*, p. 202.

regarded as philosophically absurd, and Szymanowski argued for a system which permitted a child to proceed to

> elevated religious spheres (a fundamental sense of God, eternity and the fathomless depths of conscious life), not from this continually shame-faced ethical side – with its constant emphasis on the sexual aspect and the transgression of apodictic regulations [...]. In a word, to show religion not as an institution imposing obligations and conjuring up a complex mirage [one illegible word] of happiness, the apodictic antithesis of life, but as a force spreading to the furthest bounds of the inner life of the soul, answerable to itself for its own qualities.[59]

Similar pre-occupations run throughout 'The Tale of the Miracle of the Youth Enoch Porfiry, Iconographer', purportedly a sample of Łowicki's own work and in effect a lyrical expression of some of the theorising to be found in the 'Symposium'. At almost every point of the tale, there are further parallels with *King Roger*. There are the opulent descriptions of Byzantium and the Palermo of Roger II, and indeed the opening paragraphs are almost a 'dry run' for the opera with their evocation of the

> dim gold light of candles mingling with the trailing smoke of incense, and the gloomy sound [...] of monks chanting [...] 'Holy, holy, holy' [...] before the face of the Living God – Jesus Christ – of whom a terrible likeness with emaciated face, black beard and unfathomable, undivining eyes loomed menacingly in the flickering light of the candelabras, like a dead spectre lurking amidst the tarnished gold of the mosaic adorning the high vault of the apse.[60]

Again the tale is fundamentally to do with the clash between Judaeo-Christianity and Hellenism and the revelation of the relationship between Christ and Eros. Enoch Porfiry, a novice in the monastery of St Athanasius in the town of Nikomedia in Bythynia, is an iconographer whose magical hands created mosaics of such marvellous beauty of colour and shape that the pious brothers in the monastery suspected him of a pact with the Prince of Darkness. In spite of those 'venomous whispers swirling snake-like in the dark recesses of the monastery',[61] it is Porfiry who is selected to travel to Byzantium and thence to Palermo to assist in the decoration of a newly built shrine. He is to be accompanied by Brother Simeon, who embodies the forces of orthodoxy. Simeon is the monastery's treasurer and had come from Tarsus, in which fact he took exceeding pride, 'harbouring in his gloomy fanatical soul a deep cult for the blessed apostle and martyr Paul'.[62]

---

[59] *Ibid.*, p. 202.
[60] *Ibid.*, p. 169.
[61] *Ibid.*, p. 171.
[62] *Ibid.*, p. 171.

At the start of the tale, Porfiry is fearful of his own forbidding mosaics of Christ, in the creation of which he had 'called into being his own mortal dread and terror in the fearful, unfathomable abyss of those dark eyes which gazed searchingly into the most secret depths of his being'.[63] But in Palermo Porfiry encounters the 'God of Love' in the form of a beautiful youth, on whose lips a smile of indescribable sweetness appeared. He entrusts his deepest secrets to Porfiry, who hangs with 'unassuageable yearning on words which [...] encircled him like a happy, joyous, fluttering garland of butterflies'.[64] Porfiry is seized by an indomitable urge to act and, as dawn breaks, he locks himself into the partly completed shrine to the Holy Mother. As it is a Sunday, the day of rest for all the other artists, he is able to labour without interruption on the vault above the proposed site of the altar. By evening, instead of a terrible image of the crucified one, there is 'a faithful likeness of Eros risen from the dead – the God of Love, who [...] had revealed himself that very night to the eyes and heart of Porfiry in the form of a real figure, pulsating with life'.[65] In the prayer which Porfiry subsequently addresses to the wooden crucifix, it becomes clear that he now believes he has discovered the divine truth of the equation of Christ and Eros, through the creation of a true likeness of his lord. But catastrophe soon ensues, for the pious brethren break into the shrine and Simeon, enraged at Porfiry's blasphemy, stabs him. Angels take the mortal remains of Porfiry up to heaven, and in place of the image of Eros with which Porfiry had decorated the vault, there remained only his own saintly likeness, showing him as he was in the hour of his martyr's death, 'eyes shining full of the deepest secret which [...] the lips of the Crucified one had vouchsafed to him in a whisper'.[66] As for Simeon,

> the Lord God [...] ordained him in madness to take his own life, for as Judas Iscariot once did, so too did Simeon of Tarsus, who was discovered hanging by the neck from a sycamore tree growing close by the church. Infinite is God's justice and compassion.[67]

A further set of influences on the ideology of *King Roger* can be traced to the poetry and dramas of the 'Young Poland in Literature' writer, Tadeusz Miciński. As has already been observed, links existed between Miciński and Szymanowski at all stages of the composer's career, from the early settings of poetry from *W mroku gwiazd* ('In the twilight of the stars'), in Four

[63] *Ibid.*, p. 171.
[64] *Ibid.*, p. 178.
[65] *Ibid.*, p. 181.
[66] *Ibid.*, p. 186.
[67] *Ibid.*, p. 186.

Songs, Op. 11, and Six Songs, Op. 20, the setting of Miciński's translation of Djalal ad-Dīn Rūmī in the Third Symphony, the programmatic bases of both the *Concert Overture*, Op. 12, and the First Violin Concerto, Op. 35,[68] and finally the incidental music for the drama *Kniaź Patiomkin* ('Prince Potemkin'), dating from 1925. Teresa Chylińska has shown that *King Roger* demonstrates the long-lasting impact on Szymanowski of Miciński's drama *Bazilissa Teofanu*, dating from 1909, 'one of the most original works of Polish theatre, unusual for its intellectual novelty, scenic solutions, handling of crowd scenes, the play of movement and light.'[69]

Like *King Roger* this drama is a series of tableaux set in the mediaeval world, in this case tenth-century Constantinople. There are further obvious parallels with *King Roger*, namely the religious ideology, the mixture of Byzantine and Norman culture, Greek mythology, and in particular a central character attempting to confront the Dionysian within herself. The Polish theatrical director, Leon Schiller, who worked with Szymanowski, subsequently reported that the composer valued this play in particular as he believed that it constituted a new form for Polish monumental drama. There are indeed extraordinary concordances between the opening scene of the opera and that of Miciński's play. Both open with a liturgical scene, that of *Bazillisa Teofanu* being characterised by Miciński in the following terms:

> Above the quiet, collective, litanied whispers of the crowd, swells a choir of bass-voices, and a hymn on organ links this with the majesty of the soul reflecting over the dark secrets of mortal life and the resurrection of the dead.[70]

After the curtain rises, a monastic hymn is heard:

> In the gloomy heavens of your mysteries, Lord, are reflected the Candlemas candles of our hearts, guide us, Kyrie Eleison! You rule the Earth, you descend to hell (to the devils), you lead the weary soul to paradise – O Jesus – Jesus – vanquisher of death.[71]

Finally, there are Miciński's scenic directions for this tableau, which are reminiscent not only of Szymanowski's own for *King Roger*, but also some of the opulent imagery deployed in 'The Tale of Enoch Porfiry':

---

[68] The *Concert Overture* was initially linked with the poem 'Witeź Włast' ('Włast the Knight') and the First Violin Concerto with 'Noc majowa' ('May Night'); *cf.* p. 35, above.

[69] Teresa Chylińska, 'Karol Szymanowski i Tadeusz Miciński' ('Karol Szymanowski and Tadeusz Miciński'), in Maria Podraza-Kwiatkowska (ed.), *Studia o Tadeuszu Micińskim* ('Studies on Tadeusz Miciński'), Wydawnictwo Literackie, Kraków, 1979, p. 332.

[70] *Ibid.*, p. 335.

[71] *Ibid.*, p. 335.

The interior of the Myrandrion Church – through stained-glass windows with golden colours and dark smokey violet, burning scarlet and calmer green – chromatic broken lights merge with the gloom, creating together with the church one wild sorcery of a mosaic. The Hyperagia Mother of God, her head shrouded in gloom, its huge shape hidden in the depths of the vault; in the blazing candelabras, lamps and chandeliers the embroidery of jewels on her robe stands out. The tiles of mottled marble, whose wavy lines imitate a stormy sea – a splendid colonnade of green verde antico marbles taken from the temple of Diana of Ephesus, the Phrygian white with streaks of blood from the beautiful Attys, the Libyan azure, Egyptian granite, black Celtic pylons – and on the ground, the mighty sarcophagi of the dead Caesars.

Thousands of glittering lights, reflections of mosaics, the lustre of crystals, golden shields – all marvels, which create on the ground the dying sun of ancient civilizations, are lost in the gloomy abyss of the Apocalyptic Cosmos: there on the walls and in the blue stone the Jerusalem army of saints in petrified ecstasy – long-bodied, astral shapes – exhausted – in eternal silence. Religious creatures – drinking at springs, sheep, peacocks and ring-doves amidst sycamores, on grape-vines the beast from Ezekiel's vision with the seven heads and ten crowns – Greek centaurs amongst the woods....[72]

The parallels between Miciński's directions and those of Szymanowski are obvious, and it is again fascinating to observe how the composer not only continued to hide himself away in this exotic, imaginary world long after he had escaped from the Ukraine, but quite deliberately reverted to a 'Young Poland' creative landscape at this stage of his career. No doubt it arose in part as a defence mechanism when he had to cope with the American way of life he encountered in the course of his trip to the United States in 1921. The extent of his disenchantment becomes abundantly clear from a draft of a letter to Iwaszkiewicz:

the strangeness, the hostility even of the culture here simply overwhelms me and I am far – oh so far – from any sort of feeling of happiness. At the most sometimes gratification of this or that pleasure, and in the long run, just the immediate warmth of one's dearest ones – the Kochańskis and Artur [Rubinstein]! My pessimism concerning the essential values of the New World is not deep, but not without foundation. [...] I am closing myself away in myself [...] and am stifling the typical contempt of the incurable, old-fashioned European.[73]

When not clandestinely abusing the locals in the company of fellow Europeans, Szymanowski busied himself with various creative projects, which again had more to do with literature than music. Apart from the

---

[72] *Ibid.*, pp. 334–35.
[73] Draft dated 15 March 1921, in *Karol Szymanowski Korespondencja*, Vol. 2, *op. cit.*, p. 216.

revisions to the libretto of *King Roger*, he started, but failed to complete, two novels. 'Tomek' is a humorous depiction of the collision of American and European values and cultures, whereas 'The Tale of the Wandering Juggler and the Seven Stars' represents Szymanowski's final flight from reality to the sort of escapism to which he had resorted during the war years. In some measure, the juggler himself shows certain similarities with Pater's Denis. He is a mysterious solitary, who having 'no name and no home, led no existence amongst mankind,'[74] singing his 'unsingable songs to no-one but himself'.[75] He composes strange fairy-tales, smiling at his tiny works undertaken for his own amusement. He also considers himself handsome and delights in seeing 'his shining eyes, red ruby lips and the youthful suppleness of his limbs'[76] reflected in the unruffled surface of sleepy forest lakes. He comes into contact with an Unknown One, a latter-day Narcissus:

> By the shore-side a youth, unknown to him, was resting on the sand, quiet and motionless. He seemed to be asleep – his elbows rested on the ground, his head cradled in his palms and he seemed to be gazing fixedly into the depths of the still waters. [...] the Unknown One slowly turned his head in a lazy, off-hand manner, and shot a glance at the juggler who stopped a few paces away. Silence fell again. Their eyes met, and it could have been an instant or a whole hour that passed, for time became lost in that silence, [...] leaving nothing in the soul of the juggler apart from the terrible certainty, full of unknown sweetness, that the face of the Unknown One was the single, the only expression of sublime, indescribable Beauty that he had ever encountered. [...] a joy, hitherto unfamiliar to him, pulsated through his heart when, unexpectedly, a smile like a volatile, inconstant, faint glow of an inner fire appeared on the youth's exquisite, fresh lips.[77]

This extract from 'The Juggler' was Szymanowski's final (recorded) vision of the beautiful, smiling ephebe, this one so enfeebled, however, that he can scarcely summon up the energy to tear his eyes away from his own reflection, still less run Dionysian riot. It is no surprise to find that this most flaccid and self-indulgent of the composer's homo-erotic fantasies petered out at this point, but if nothing else it throws into sharp relief the successful confrontation of this tendency effected in the revised ending of the final act of *King Roger*. In place of Iwaszkiewicz's proposed world-renunciation, represented by Roger's whole-hearted subjection of himself to the will of the shepherd, Szymanowski introduced a much more ambiguous tone to the conclusion. Following the final appearance of the shepherd as Dionysus,

[74] *Karol Szymanowsi Pisma*, Vol. 2, *op. cit.*, p. 312.
[75] *Ibid.*, p. 313.
[76] *Ibid.*, p. 313.
[77] *Ibid.*, p. 315.

Roger and his Arab sage are left alone on stage, deserted by the rest of the
court who follow the shepherd into his 'rapturous eternal land'. As dawn
breaks, Roger clambers to the top of the theatre, itself plunged in livid-blue
darkness whereas he himself is brilliantly lit, and after singing his hymn to
the rising sun, stretches out the palms of his hands, as if bearing in them a
priceless gift.

Teresa Chylińska has remarked that this conclusion is not so much 'an
ending but only a suggestion',[78] and has discussed the symbolism of the sun,
and in particular its connection with the ideology of the 'Young Poland'
literary movement:

> At the base of Young Poland's 'solarism' – besides the search for new
> transcendentalism – lies the collective will [...] of might and happiness.
> The sun was at times a symbol of collective yearning for national freedom
> and social justice, and at times individual, 'psychological'. The yearning
> for the sun indicated in this last instance an aspiration to the unattainable
> ideal, archetypal Paradise Lost. The 'sun of mankind', 'sun of brotherhood',
> 'sun-life' – a multi-vocal indicator of spiritual freedom and a liberation of
> thought.[79]

Chylińska also emphasises the constant presence of Miciński within
Szymanowski's imaginative poetic world, and the fact that the appearance
of the symbol of the sun in Miciński's poetry encompassed the syncretic
religious symbol of the 'Sun-Christ' and signs of spiritual renewal and
inner strength, primarily of the individual, but also in collective, national
terms: 'Miciński was, one might say, the priest who restored anew the sun-
myth, the religion of the sun'.[80] In this context, it is especially significant that
Bazyllisa Teofanu, like *King Roger*, closes with solar references:

> Love me and the sun, my children, and if it is difficult for you to do this at any
> time – then just the Sun![81]

For Chylińska, Szymanowski's imagination was affected by the religious
syncretism of 'Young Poland in Literature', and 'the sacral sun was evidence,
although in a more concealed form, of a longing for faith, search for a
divinity and a need to experience religion and to recover one's sense'.[82]

---

[78] *Karol Szymanowski: His Life and Work, op. cit.*, p. 186.
[79] *Ibid.*, p. 186.
[80] *Ibid.*, p. 186.
[81] Tadeusz Miciński, *W mrokach złotego Pałacu czyli Bazilissa Teofanu. Tragedja z dziejów Bizancjum X. wieku* ('In the gloom of the golden Palace or Bazilla Teofanu. A Tragedy from the history of 10th-century Byzantium'), Drukarnia Uniwersytetu Jagiellońskiego, Kraków, 1909, p. 238.
[82] *Ibid.*, p. 186.

It is fundamentally with 'recovering sense' that *King Roger* is concerned. Perhaps the most striking image of Roger's hymn to the rising sun, inserted by Szymanowski himself, is that of sails unfurling like white wings of gulls: 'The wings grow! They encompass the whole world.'[83] Wing-imagery is almost a poetic leitmotif for Szymanowski: it occurs throughout his writings, and with particular frequency in *Efebos*. At its simplest, it appears at the start of 'The Tale of Enoch Porfiry' when Porfiry is pictured on board the ship speeding him to Byzantium, 'its white sails extended like a swan's wings.'[84] A little later, Porfiry's dreams and recollections sing to him like birds returned to freedom, flying like the white gulls accompanying the ship, 'the soundless beat of their wings overtaking him.'[85] Towards the climax of the tale, as Porfiry struggles to express his understanding of the equation of Christ-Eros, he speaks of his soul flying 'to dwell at your feet for the first time like a free bird, flying aloft on broad white wings.'[86]

Elsewhere, wings and flight are associated with the highest aspirations of mankind. The wings of Icarus are mentioned in the course of the 'Symposium' by Rellov in connection with the (perhaps doomed) quest for the secrets of love and beauty in the face of the 'pride and vanity of a soulless, mechanical culture as never previously existed'[87] – remarks which in themselves recall sentiments expressed by Thomas Carlyle almost a hundred years earlier in 'Signs of the Times', an essay published in June 1829 in *The Edinburgh Review* and still one of the most effective critiques of nineteenth-century materialism. Still more significant is the allusion to the imagery of wings in Rellov's paraphrase of a passage from Plato's *Phaedrus*: 'And again they wander along luminous tracks – and at the great moment, they grow wings, so as to be able to love.'[88] For Plato, it was essential for the soul to grow wings because the wing raised what was heavy into the region above, where the gods dwell: of all things connected with the body, it has the greatest affinity with the divine, which is endowed with beauty, wisdom, goodness and every other excellence. These qualities are the prime source of nourishment and growth to the wing of the soul, but their opposites, such as ugliness and evil, cause the wings to waste and perish.[89]

But though love could lead to the growth of wings, the higher elements in the minds of the lovers had to prevail, guiding them in the pursuit of

[83] Karol Szymanowski, *Król Roger*, Complete Edition, Vol. 14, PWM, Kraków, 1973, pp. 308-9.
[84] *Karol Szymanowsi Pisma*, Vol. 2, *op. cit.*, p. 170.
[85] *Ibid.*, p. 174.
[86] *Ibid.*, p. 182.
[87] *Ibid.*, p. 163.
[88] Plato, *Phaedrus*, transl. Walter Hamilton, Penguin, Harmondsworth, 1973, p. 51.
[89] *Ibid.*, p. 65.

wisdom, so that 'by subduing the part of the soul that contained the seeds of vice and setting free that in which virtue had its birth they become masters of themselves and their souls will be at peace'.[90] It followed then that those who practised a less exalted way of life, failing to master themselves, would 'emerge from the body without wings'.[91]

In *King Roger*, the winning of wings is achieved through what Rellov, elsewhere in the 'Symposium', described as 'liberation from the almighty power of natural, primitive instincts',[92] a process which necessarily entails a recognition and right co-ordination of the forces which make up the human psyche. In truth, *King Roger* is the work of one of a long line of thinkers concerned with this most fundamental problem for mankind, a line running from Plato, with his allegorical comparison of the soul with the winged charioteer and his pair of horses, one 'fine and good and of noble stock, and the other the opposite in every way',[93] through to a series of nineteenth-century writings, some of which undoubtedly underpinned the ideology of the opera. In *Conversations with Eckermann* – one of two works which Szymanowski told Iwaszkiewicz were 'the most beautiful books in the world',[94] the other being Nietzsche's *The Birth of Tragedy* – Goethe speaks of the importance of mastering what he described as the Daemonic, a secret, problematic power, chiefly manifest in art, 'which all men feel, which no philosopher explains, and over which the religious help themselves with consoling words'.[95] For Goethe, whose *Faust* was an investigation of just such a theme, this power could not be explained by reason or understanding: 'it lies not in my nature, but I am subject to it, it manifests itself in a thoroughly active power'.[96]

In that other 'most beautiful book in the world', Nietzsche's *Birth of Tragedy*, there is a vivid characterisation of Dionysus as the antithesis of Apollo, in other words, as a life-force tending against what Schopenhauer described as the *principium individuationis*, expressed most forcefully in corporate song and dance:

> Under the influence of the Dionysian, not only is the union between man and man reaffirmed, but nature which has become alienated, hostile or subjugated, celebrates once more her reconciliation with her lost son, man. [...] Now the

[90] *Ibid.*, p. 65.

[91] *Ibid.*, p. 65.

[92] *Karol Szymanowsi Pisma*, Tom 2, *op. cit.*, p. 154.

[93] *Op. cit.*, p. 51.

[94] Iwaszkiewicz, 'Szymanowscy' ('The Szymanowskis') from 'Książki moich wspomnień' ('The Book of my Reminiscences'), 1957, in *Karol Szymanowski we wspomnieniach, op. cit.*, p. 19.

[95] *Conversations with Eckermann*, transl. John Oxenford, Geo. Bell & Sons, London, 1901, p. 525.

[96] *Ibid.*, p. 525.

slave is a free man, now all the rigid hostile barriers that necessity, caprice, or 'hostile convention' have fixed between man and man are broken. Now with the gospel of universal harmony, each one feels himself not only united, reconciled, and fused with his neighbour, but as one within him, as if the veil of maya had been torn aside and was now fluttering in tatters before the mysterious primordial unity.

In song and dance man expresses himself as a member of a higher community; he has forgotten how to walk and speak and is on the way toward flying in the air, dancing. His very gestures express enchantment. [...] he feels himself a god, he himself now walks about enchanted, in ecstasy, like the gods he saw walking in his dreams.[97]

It has to be admitted from the outset that this extract serves to underscore only the earlier stages of *King Roger*, representing a confrontation of vital life-forces with hieratical systems of church and state. As has been observed, Szymanowski felt unable to endorse the return to the old gods initially proposed by Iwaszkiewicz. In this respect he approached much more closely the underlying message of *The Bacchae*, where vital, instinctual forces are clearly not to be ignored, but neither are they to be allowed free reign. The fate of Pentheus, torn to shreds by maenads led by his own mother, dispels any attraction the flight from reason to the old gods may have had. Indeed, Nietzsche's own view of the Dionysian was gradually modified, and it is a passage from one of his final works – *Twilight of the Idols or How to Philosophise with a Hammer* – which best encapsulates in brief the ideology of *King Roger* and in so doing, throws light on the ambiguous final scene. The passage in question is a characterisation of Goethe as a truly Dionysian man in so far as he

conceived of a strong, highly cultured human being who, keeping himself in check and having reverence for himself, dares to allow himself the whole compass and wealth of naturalness, but who is strong enough for this freedom; a man of tolerance, not out of weakness, but out of strength, because he knows how to employ to his advantage what would destroy an average nature; a man to whom nothing is forbidden, except it be weakness, whether that weakness be called vice or virtue....

A spirit thus *emancipated* stands in the midst of the universe with a joyful and trusting fatalism, in the *faith* that only what is separate and individual may be rejected, that in the totality everything is redeemed and affirmed – *he no longer denies*. ... But such a faith is the highest of all possible faiths: I have baptised it with the name *Dionysus*.[98]

---

[97] Friedrich Nietzsche, *The Birth of Tragedy*, translated by Walter Kaufmann. New York 1967, p. 37.
[98] Friedrich Nietzsche, *Twilight of the Idols or How to Philosophize with a Hammer*, translated by R.J. Hollingdale. Penguin, Harmondsworth, 1968, p. 103.

This Dionysian creative force is only possible in one who has overcome himself and recognised and mastered those passions represented by the Dionysus of old. In more mundane, but no less illuminating, Jungian terms, development of the whole personality depends on the successful integration of the dark forces or the 'shadow', here represented by the Shepherd, even though this process brings with it 'the conscious and unavoidable segregation of the single individual from the undifferentiated and unconscious herd'.[99]

Szymanowski himself understood that segregation was almost inevitably the price to be paid in the search for wholeness. It is evident in both Roger's splendid isolation at the close of the opera and in the aggressively aristocratic tone of *Efebos*. It has to be said, however, that though *Efebos* casts illuminating shafts of light on the composer's ideology, its self-conscious elitism is symptomatic of an intermittent failure to transcend its escapist origins and to maintain the balance and (self-)control that distinguishes *King Roger*. The opera, for all its ambiguity, is one of the few works of the twentieth century which confronts directly the problem of making humankind whole, and as such is one of those select music-dramas that may genuinely be regarded as a philosophical, psychological and even, in the broadest and best sense of the word, a religious document. Its composition was not intended as a money-spinning or career-enhancing project – as had been the case with *Lottery for Husbands* and *Hagith*: Szymanowski regarded its composition as a question of his further artistic existence, and as Teresa Chylińska has remarked, the opera came to embody 'the centrepiece, the crossing point indicating his most essential aesthetic, philosophic, psychological, stylistic and technical tendencies'.[100]

[99] C. G. Jung, *The Development of the Personality*, Routledge, London, 1954, p. 172.
[100] Teresa Chylińska, *Karol Szymanowski: His Life and Works*, University of Southern California, Los Angeles, 1993, p. 184.

V
The Music
of the Opera

From a musical point of view, *King Roger* can be regarded as the climax of what might be termed Szymanowski's 'middle' period, roughly coinciding with the years of the First World War. The preceding era had been marked by an intense development of Germanic styles and methods, typified by the Second Symphony, Op. 19 (1909–10), Second Piano Sonata, Op. 21 (1910–11), and the Straussian one-act opera *Hagith*, Op. 25 (1912–13). From 1914, however, he set about 'mediterraneanising' his music, and in the process created a supra-European, hedonistic art which, in the words of Nietzsche, one of his favourite philosophers,

> does not fade away at the voluptuous blue sea and the brightness of the Mediterranean sky, nor [...] turn yellow and then pale as all German music does [...]. [Its] rarest magic would consist in its no longer knowing anything of good and evil [...].[1]

The earliest works to reflect this new approach, in which a rapprochement between high-tension chromatic harmony, intricate thematic working and an expanded range of timbre is effected, are the second series of *Des Hafis Liebeslieder*, Op. 26, for voice and orchestra (1914) – the first series of *Des Hafis Liebeslieder*, Op. 24, written some three years earlier had been for voice and piano; *Métopes*, Op. 29 (1915), three poems for solo piano; and *Mythes*, Op. 30 (1915), three poems for violin and piano. The first of these works drew on paraphrases by Hans Bethge of verses by the Persian poet, Hafiz of Shiraz (d. 1390), the two instrumental works on Greek mythology. Both sets of *Des Hafis Liebeslieder* provide evidence of Szymanowski's fascination with oriental subject-matter, and his work increasingly bore traits of a subtle stylisation of features of Arabic music. Arabic features can be detected in many works of these years, notably the Third Symphony, Op. 29 (1916), which incorporated settings of texts by the Persian Sufist poet, Mevlāna Jalal ad-Dīn Rūmī (1207–73); *Songs of the Fairytale Princess*,

---

[1] Friedrich Nietzsche, *Beyond Good and Evil*, translated by W. Kaufmann, Vintage, New York, 1966, p. 195.

Op. 31 (1915), to words by his sister, Zofia Szymanowska; *Songs of the Infatuated Muezzin*, Op. 42 (1918), to words by Jarosław Iwaszkiewicz, and not least, *King Roger*, and in particular Roksana's song in the Second Act. Orientalism here contributed much to the authenticity of the opera. So, too, did the use of medieval organum at the start of the piece where, whether consciously or not, Szymanowski seemed to find his way to express the essence of Byzantine chant.

King Roger is rightly regarded as one of the most important works in the Polish operatic repertory and, like such more obviously nationalistic works as Moniuszko's *Halka* (1847) and *Straszny Dwór* ('The Haunted Manor'; 1864), is regularly performed in Poland. It has also largely eclipsed other Polish operatic works of the early years of the twentieth century – for example, Paderewski's *Manru* and Różycki's *Bolesław Śmiały* ('Boleslaw the Bold'; 1908), *Casanova* (1922) and *Beatrix Cenci* (1926). Within Szymanowski's own output, *King Roger* marked a retreat from the self-consciously 'modernist' stance adopted in *Hagith*, with its Straussian one-act design and limited use of *Sprechgesang*. It is cast in three acts, but though the music plays continuously, there are a number of *parlando* and *arioso* passages, mainly used for outlining the narrative (the equivalent of the recitative of earlier opera) as distinct from the more lyrical, self-contained moments. There is some use of leitmotif, but the dramatically static nature of much of the writing is more redolent of the tableau-like approach of some Russian national composers (notably Mussorgsky) than Wagner. To some extent, this dramatic method is comparable with that of Handelian oratorio, and like Handel, Szymanowski laid considerable emphasis on the chorus as representative of the people. Prominent choral passages are to be found in all three acts, with additionally a boys' choir in the first. In both First and Third Acts, solo voices within the chorus are allotted prominent roles. Otherwise, the opera requires only six solo singers, two of whom – the Archiereios (Archbishop; bass) and Deaconess (contralto) – have relatively minor roles in the First Act. The role of Roger is sung by a baritone, that of his consort Roksana by a soprano and those of the Arabian Sage Edrisi and the Shepherd by tenors.

The instrumentation is richly textured and often polyphonically complex, and Szymanowski had recourse to a full 'post-Romantic' orchestra comprising:

three flutes (one doubling piccolo)
three oboes (one doubling cor anglais)
three clarinets
one bass clarinet
three bassoons (one doubling contrabassoon)

four horns
four off-stage trumpets
three further trumpets
three trombones and tuba
timpani
tamburo piccolo
tamburo basco
bass drum
triangle
cymbals
tam-tam
xylophone
bells
celeste
two harps
piano
organ
strings

Act One

The opening act, according to Szymanowski's scenic notes, is set within a church erected by the omnipotent Byzantine Basilei, the former rulers of the island:

> Upstage, in the middle, is a huge semi-circular apse vaulted over the high altar, which is separated from the nave by a row of small columns of mottled marble, the tops of which are crowned by various strange figures. In the middle, wide-open gates reveal a flight of steps leading to the altar, bedecked with glowing candles. The numerous arches and vaults of the church are supported by columns of heavy stone, plundered from the ruins of ancient temples. The interior of the dome of the apse is covered with a gigantic mosaic icon of Christ with lean ascetic face, unfathomable black eyes, right hand ominously raised, and on either side, in attendance, are angels, pensive, absorbed in prayer. The general background of dim, tarnished gold glitters lazily in the light of thousands of candles glowing in the candelabras suspended from the ceiling. The side arches and vaults are also covered with various detailed and sumptuously coloured mosaics, representing scenes from the lives of the Apostles SS. Peter and Paul.
>
> The broken rhythm of the church results from the influences of later invaders and rulers of the island. A part of the ceiling, fashioned in wood by Arab craftsmen, takes the form of sumptuously coloured stalactites, on which skilfully placed verses from the Koran can be seen in Cufic script. Such a ceiling can still be seen in the Capella Palatina in the palace of the Sicilian

kings at Palermo. Four stone lions are placed half-way up the walls. The pulpit and the floor are decorated with rich marble mosaics.

The singing of a hymn can be heard before the curtain rises slowly. The stage, lit only by a large number of candles and the last rays of the setting sun, is partly obscured in gloom. Although the church is full of people, it seems to be quite still. Dark figures of monks and nuns are seen kneeling with heads bowed. Conspicuous among the nuns is the tall figure of the Deaconess. The Archiereios in a golden robe stands in front of the altar. A crowd of deacons, presbyters and acolytes can be seen behind the row of small columns. The only movement is that of slowly swinging thuribles [a censer in which incense is burnt].

The crowd remain motionless until the King and his court enter the church.[2]

The opera moves from sunset, through darkest night to glorious sunrise, and thus it is that the admittedly exquisite atrophy of the opening evocation of the medieval church is symbolically bathed in the rays of a sinking sun. The hymn heard at the outset, initially unaccompanied save for a soft tam-tam, is the Sanctus, originally sung by seraphims around the throne of God in the vision of the prophet Isaiah.[3] There is no evidence to suggest that Szymanowski systematically studied the music of the Byzantine rite, the rite which would have been employed in the Sicilian church during the reign of Roger II, and yet the opening melodic line, which generates much of the thematic material for the First Act, is identical to the second authentic mode of Byzantine chant, the Neanes Echos (Ex. 1) – although Szymanowski's treatment, of course, goes far beyond the monophony of plainchant.

Ex. 1

First heard is an organum in fifths, and then denser harmonisations involving triads which, though continuing to evoke a mediaeval atmosphere, swing anachronistically from the key of B minor to its dominant, F sharp (Ex. 2). Appearances of the Neanes Echos are labelled *x*. In place of the constant melodic variation and elaboration which characterise Byzantine chant, Szymanowski constantly contrasts registers and textural densities, employing up to nine separate vocal strands on occasion plus a boys' choir of three to four parts.

[2] Karol Szymanowski, *King Roger*, Collected Edition Vol. 14, PWM, Kraków, 1973, p. XIV.
[3] 'I saw also the Lord sitting upon a throne, high and lifted up, and his train filled the temple. Above it stood the seraphims [...] and one cried unto another and said, Holy, holy, holy is the Lord of hosts; the whole earth is full of his glory' (Isaiah, 6: 1–3).

The Music of the Opera

Ex. 2

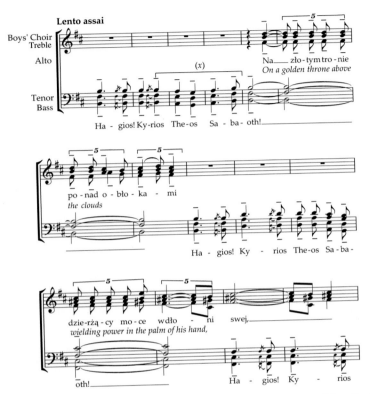

Throughout, the hymn underlines the power and awfulness of the Godhead. The Archiereios, accompanied by *bocca chiusa* voices, sings of the presence of God in the burning bush, in thunderbolts on Mount Sinai, in raging winds (Ex. 3); the boys refer to God on a golden throne above the clouds, cherubims and seraphims, powers and principalities prostrating themselves before him as, wielding a flaming sword, he despatches his archangels to do his will.

Ex. 3

Additional instrumental support is provided by the organ, playing single pedal notes, and timpani along with intermittent notes on triangle. The other instruments of the orchestra are introduced only at the close of the hymn as Roger enters, attended by his court, the first movement on stage since the curtain rose. Immediately, the apparent certainties of the medieval world are seemingly thrown into question as the primitive sounds of the opening give way to a luxurious, more complex sound. It signals the presence of a more advanced consciousness, less dependent on externally imposed dogma. This more questioning outlook is further underlined by the inversion of the opening melody, (*x*) in Ex. 1, now rising and falling with earth-bound effect, and a harmonisation, laced with whole-tone elements, that is tonally ambivalent (Ex. 4).

Ex. 4

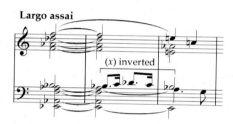

This passage is anchored to an E flat pedal, giving way to an unambiguous C major as the people acclaim their king. The opening motive, in triadic organum over pedal C, forms the basis for this acclamation which takes a form similar to that of the acclamations to be found in Byzantine ceremonial. Such so-called *euphemia* were traditionally performed by two groups of singers in antiphony – a practice followed by Szymanowski in so far as the main acclamation is repeated by a solo tenor and boys' choir. There is also a marked similarity with the structure of Byzantine acclamation, which consists of three main sections: a liturgical formula ('May the Lord God from everlasting to everlasting bless our king'), the names of the ruler and his consort in the simplest possible repeated-note style ('Roger and his noble consort'), followed by a final liturgical formula ('May God bless them!').[4]

The unambiguous nature of the music of the acclamation is indication enough of the power and esteem the king enjoys, and it is to this mighty, self-appointed vicar of Christ on earth that the Archiereios and Deaconess address their pleas. In music of vicious simplicity, entirely lacking in the archaic charm of the opening minutes of the opera, they urge Roger to protect the faith. They tell him that a shepherd has been stirring up the people and leading them astray, turning them against the faith and, as the deaconess is keen to point out, inciting young women to sin. The crowd joins

[4] *Cf.* Egon Wellesz, *Byzantine Music and Hymnography*, Oxford University Press, Oxford, 1961, p. 98.

in urging the king to judge their 'unfathomable transgressions'. Roger turns to his companion, the Arabian sage Edrisi, a symbol throughout the opera of rational enquiry, and asks in lowered tones, what he has heard (Ex. 5).

Ex. 5

Thus, in this telling contrast of outward temporal might and inward uncertainty, economically revealed in shifting, chromatic harmonies, and the nervously striving lines that accompany his question, Szymanowski reveals all that the listener has to know about Roger for the present.

Edrisi informs Roger that the Shepherd is rumoured to be roaming the island, teaching strange things and singing strange songs in praise of an unknown god. The delicate arabesque lines in the accompanying cor anglais anticipate the opening melody of the Shepherd's Dionysian dance-song of the Second Act (Ex. 6).

Ex. 6

The Archiereios and Deaconess complain that that very day he dared to speak to the people before the church, promulgating evil as he departed. He should be imprisoned. Roksana, the king's consort, reminds Roger that he is committed to justice, and that he should at least hear what the Shepherd has to say. Her melody, like Edrisi's, is more lyrical and wide-ranging, but its luxuriant and tonally indeterminate harmonic support reveals a more instinctive, volatile nature. Woven into her line, and accompanying figuration, is a cell of semitone and minor third or augmented second (*y*), which will feature prominently in her celebrated aria in the Second Act.[5]

---

[5] It had already been used by Szymanowski in other works, notably the First Violin Concerto of 1916 and 'The Grave of Hafiz' (from *Songs of Hafiz*, Op. 26) in 1914, where it has clear oriental connotations.

Ex. 7

Edrisi agrees with Roksana and, after a moment's thought, Roger resolutely orders the Shepherd to be brought before him. The crowd offer unsolicited advice; as before, their pleas that Roger should punish the blaspheming Shepherd take the form of obsessively repeated patterns. Roger silences them with an impatient gesture, and goes on to ask Edrisi for more information about the Shepherd. He is told that he is young, has curly, copper-coloured hair and is dressed in a goatskin, like every shepherd. He has eyes like stars, and a smile full of mystery. Wider-spanning 'oriental' arabesques accompany Edrisi's description, and his motif is taken up by Roksana (Ex. 8) as she pensively reflects on the Shepherd's smile, full of mystery, akin to that hidden from the sun in the limpid depths of forest lakes.

Ex. 8

This passage is anchored to a pedal on A, supporting chromatically shifting lines embedded in a richly variegated texture, which continues to employ divided strings. Both upper strings and vocal line soar ever higher, underlining Roksana's increasing fascination with the Shepherd. In marked contrast, Roger's question as to who is the unknown God the Shepherd praises is markedly narrower in range, though still accompanied by the sinuous lines which had previously accompanied Roksana. As Edrisi tells the king he will soon hear directly from the shepherd himself, there is movement at the church doors. Agitated whispers are heard from the people, demanding the Shepherd be stoned and burned in oil. This passage, built on ostinati (Ex. 9), is initially in B flat minor, but latterly moves to G flat major, though still retaining the B flat pedal in the bass.

Ex. 9

U - ka-mie-no-wać,
Stone him,

A single violin sustains a high B flat that rises semitonally to form part of a chord of E major to breath-taking effect as the Shepherd enters (Ex. 10).

Ex. 10

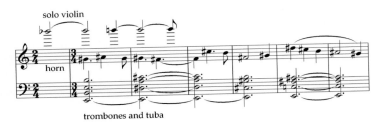

He stands at the threshold. He looks boldly at the crowd gathered around, then, gazing at Roger, he walks with a slow and easy step almost to the foot of the throne. His progress through the church is conveyed in music of some considerable luxuriance (*Lento misterioso*), its melodic line deriving in part from a generally more diatonic version of music associated with Roksana and Edrisi, its exquisite sweetness enhanced by a translucent orchestration and effortlessly high floating lines.

In response to Roger's questions, the young man describes himself as a shepherd who tells of his god, a god who is as beautiful as he is himself. His simple tonal motif (Ex. 11) is taken up in the orchestra in a more whole-tone form, as if enchantment were radiating from him.

Ex. 11

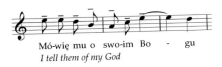

Mó-wię mu o swo-im Bo - gu
I tell them of my God

The people, Archiereios and Deaconess want him silenced, but Roger, with a commanding gesture, sweeps their demands aside and orders the Shepherd to speak. Pensively, and with an 'indescribable smile', the Shepherd begins his song, the first extended solo of the work and the structural centre-piece of the

First Act. It is characterised by a lyricism and flexibility anticipated to a degree in some of Roksana's utterances. The first of its three main sections is itself a miniature strophic song, in which the initial strain appears in different keys and with varied orchestral accompaniment. Revealingly, the opening motif is related to the *Neanes* tag of the opening ecclesiastical hymn (Ex. 1), although the variations to which it is here subjected result in a very different vibrant sound which effectively contrasts the Shepherd's pantheistic teachings with the dogmas of the established church. Nonetheless, Szymanowski's use of the same basic material points to a common source – a need for the reassurance of religion – in the human psyche.

The Shepherd tells of his god, as beautiful as he is himself: he is a good shepherd, wandering along paths and mountain tracks, seeking his stray sheep. He wears ivy wreaths and carries bunches of grapes, protecting his sheep in the middle of emerald-green pastures. The Shepherd is a votary of Dionysus, the so-called 'Lydian' god, and appropriately his opening melody, in A, is adorned with the raised fourth of the Lydian mode (Ex. 12). The music tells of an almost feminine grace, but as yet reveals nothing of the alarming power he represents. Already he seems to exert a hypnotic effect upon the people, for in spite of their hostility to him, they unconsciously begin to sing with him, and imperceptibly approach the front of the stage, closely circling the King and the Shepherd.

There is an abrupt change of pace (*subito più vivace, grazioso*) at the start of the second main section of the aria as, accompanied by glittering variations of preceding motives, the Shepherd tells of his god gazing into the waters to see his smile mirrored in the waters.[6] The Shepherd sings of the god's robes of rose-coloured light, and of his feet, strong, golden, wingless but winged, his line wistfully rising higher, delicately accompanied by largely whole-tone harmonies and harp *glissandi*. The much slower final section of the aria (*Lento*) is preceded by a passage of siren-like beauty, the generally descending drift of the melodic line bearing down into the mind, as if forcing all those listening onto a deeper, trance-like state of consciousness (Ex. 13). The Shepherd, too, seems to be absorbed by his own song, and turns abstractedly to the crowd surrounding him: he will find those who suffer, those who at night seek the hand of pleasure. He will console those who crave the sweet fruit of comfort: a great blessing slumbers in his smile! The general downward drift of the harmony (lodged over a double pedal G and D, then E and B and finally D flat and A flat) ends with an indeterminate whole-tone chord.

---

[6] A reference to the Narcissistic content of both 'Narcissus', the second of the *Mythes* for violin and piano, Op. 30 (1915), and the unfinished literary fragment, 'The Tale of the Wandering Juggler and the Seven Stars' (*cf.* p. 86, above).

Ex. 12

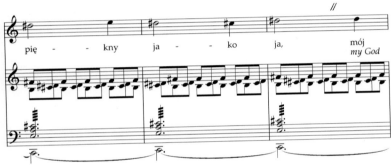

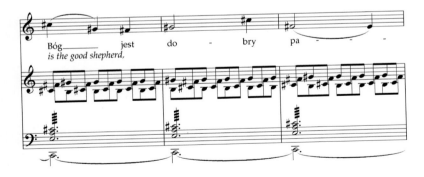

continued on p. 104

Ex. 12

continued from p. 103

sterz,_____ Przez dro - gi,_____ przez ka - mie - nie,
he wanders along stony paths and mountain tracks.

przez   ście - żki   gór   wę -

dru - - - - - je.

Ex. 13

Roksana is the first to respond to the charm of Dionysus, taking up the 'smile' motif that closed the Shepherd's song (Ex. 14). Deep in thought, and seemingly spell-bound, she repeats the shepherd's final words: 'in his smile'.

Ex. 14

She wonders what secret thrill it is that lies in the Shepherd's own eyes, like the reflection of stars on the crest of a wave, while on his lips, there is the serene smile of his God, like a glistening butterfly, poised in mid-air by a fragrant bed of scarlet roses. Gradually the melodic lines expand in range, and a richly variegated orchestral texture incorporates filigree woodwind lines, sweeping string glissandi, *sul tasto* tremolandi and harp harmonics, the whole anchored, over a lengthy pedal point. After the moment of rapt concentration at the thought of the god's smile, it is a coming back to life, but not to mundane consciousness, for Roksana has been bewitched and is now a living soul. Roger attempts to silence her, but she is swept on by the momentum of her own weirdly exultant music (Ex. 15) as she seeks to know the source of the secret fires of passion the Shepherd offers his god.

Ex. 15

Roger again interrupts: she has clearly been ensnared by the Shepherd's false witchcraft, but the Shepherd appeals to Roger to believe that he really will bring freedom to those in chains.

The people and church dignitaries now intervene. Once more they call on the king to punish the Shepherd. The Deaconess is horrified that Roksana should look on the Shepherd as a saviour, and the Archiereios points to the offence against the lifeless golden Christ above the altar. The mechanical ostinati, already associated with dogmatic faith, return, but the Shepherd seems unaware of the mounting noise and confusion, and it is he, not Roger, who interrupts the people. He tells of his god who is the shadow of green forests, the murmur of the distant sea, the storms over the ocean and the radiance of sacred eyes. His line spirals upwards in intense yearning (Ex. 16), but this time Roksana's ecstatic response is brutally cut short by Roger who, fearful of the malice in the Shepherd's eyes, orders his execution.

Ex. 16

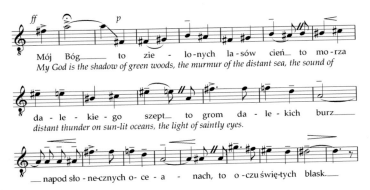

The jubilation of the people is hardly unexpected, but the glee of their diatonic, narrow-range ostinato is shocking after the luxuriance of the preceding music. Of course the blasphemer must die; God, the Almighty, the loving, the righteous, must be his judge (Ex. 17).

Ex. 17

The Shepherd, seemingly in a trance and impervious to the commotion all around, continues to sing of his god while Roksana and Edrisi both plead on his behalf. Roger orders the crowd to be silent. He slumps back on his throne. He hides his face in his hands as a terrible battle rages within him. It seems that if killing the Shepherd is not an acceptable solution, perhaps another way of avoiding confrontation would simply be to release him. Roger's agony is conveyed by a questing trombone figure, rising uncertainly only to fall back in a pathetic chromatic descent (Ex. 18).

Ex. 18

The people are stunned by this new decision, but their protests are little more than feeble wails ('Woe! He has sinned') as Roger firmly tells the crowd the Shepherd will walk free and return to the mountains (Ex. 19).

Ex. 19

A strangely beautiful smile appears on the lips of the Shepherd. He fixes his gaze on Roger, then slowly, almost hesitantly, he begins to take his leave. A new variant of the *Neanes* motif (inverted) appears (*x*), with a strongly whole-tone harmonisation (Ex. 20), underpinned by long-sustained bass notes which eventually stabilise on F sharp as Roger, with sudden resolve, orders the Shepherd to wait. That night he will stand trial. When the stars shine in the blue sky, he will come to the gates of the palace.

Ex. 20

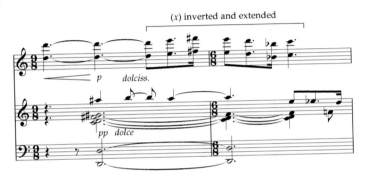

The guards will give their password – 'Shepherd' – to which the Shepherd is to reply 'Roger'. The Shepherd repeats these words, as if imprinting them on his memory, but at the same time endowing them with an additional, chilling significance as he emphasises that the King must remember that it was he himself who summoned the Shepherd to stand trial. He will come and bow down, but the King should remember – and this word sung quietly and almost unaccompanied at the apex of the Shepherd's final line – that it was he himself who instigated the trial.

There is an immediate relaxation of tension. The people continue to bewail the King's decision, but the Shepherd again takes up his song in praise of his god as he leaves. His melody is independently carried in first violins in their upper reaches, accompanied by second violins and violas, both divided in six parts, employing a variety of triplet, tremolo and tremolandi figurations. At this point the music gravitates to C, and the final sounds of the act are marked by a return to the opening organum texture ('God have mercy'), although attenuated, the pedal C and G in bass overlaid with a chord of E flat sung by the boys' choir ('Amen').

Act Two

The longest of the three acts is set in the inner courtyard of Roger's palace. Szymanowski's scenic notes indicate that the general character of the architecture show it to have been erected on the orders of the caliphs by workmen from the East, although some details indicate later accretions, wrought by the iron hand of the Norman invaders. As a result,

> the oriental softness and almost feminine refinement of the variously coloured arabesques with their subtly meandering lines, yellow-blue majolicas and rich carpets harmonise strangely with the granite arches and columns and the huge bronze entrance gate. Marvellous mosaics, the work of artists from Byzantium, shine here and there, representing mysterious gardens filled with unknown wonders and fantastic birds. Upstage, a marble fountain murmurs softly; its pool is covered by opulent flowers brought from all quarters of the globe. The courtyard is surrounded by a two-storeyed inner gallery supported by delicate columns with fantastic capitals. The main entrance, a huge bronze gate, is in the middle, upstage. Beside it is a small door curtained by a tapestry. In the upper gallery are the doors and windows of the royal harem. The gallery is connected to the stage proper by an inner flight of stairs descending on the right side. On the left, downstage, the royal throne is placed on a dais. Beside it, a little further upstage, is a huge window, half-covered by tapestry; vague outlines of trees, palms and cypresses, and a vast expanse of sky are visible through this window.[7]

Clearly, this milieu is one in which myriads of influences mingle to form the uniquely sophisticated and relatively enlightened court of this most powerful of mediaeval rulers. For Roger, who has already shown strength enough to resist suppressing the problem of the Shepherd, and with him his own inchoate desires, the trial, on the face of it, should pose no problems. The music, by contrast, reveals that what appeared to be a good idea earlier in the evening has now become a source of deep foreboding. His fear is graphically conveyed in the prelude to the act (*Molto ansioso ed agitato, ma non troppo vivace*), shot through with a troubled, brooding luxuriance and already conveying a sense that the conflict within Roger himself is becoming more explicit. A striving, whole-tone motive is linked with a violent chromatic gesture, possibly related to Roger's very first solo in the first act (Ex. 5), and a yearning semitonal figure (Ex. 21).

A sudden, mighty crescendo with a precipitous upward surge is succeeded by an equally abrupt falling-away, and hints at Roger's apprehension, his *tremor cordis* – his heart that dances, but not for joy. A new oboe theme (Ex. 22), which shares the unstable rhythmic pattern of the opening motif, leads to a complex of sensuously scored, slow-moving figures.

The King is explicitly linked to this troubled music by a recurrence of the First-Act motif that had represented his agony of indecision regarding the

---

[7] Szymanowski, *King Roger*, op. cit., 1973, p. XIV.

Ex. 21

Ex. 22

fate of the Shepherd (Ex. 18). The opening motives of the introduction are reprised as the curtain goes up.

It is night, and the courtyard is faintly lit by alabaster lamps. Attired in magnificent garments, Roger sits on the throne, while Edrisi looks through the window into the distance. Both are waiting anxiously. By the main doors, the King's guard can be seen standing motionless. According to the stage directions, Roger's whole being seems to be seized with anticipation and anxiety. He sings of the troubled stars, flickering in the green sea of heaven, and asks Edrisi to hold his burning hands in his own cold palms. He did not imagine in the confused light of day that he would be awaiting the coming of the Shepherd in such a state of fear. To this point, the music has been oppressive, but now lighter, more sinuous motives break in, the twirling, rather oriental-sounding arabesque in the oboe supported by an infectious rhythm in bass instruments and timpani (Ex. 23).

Ex. 23

Roger is roused for a moment from his dark pre-occupations, and attempts a demonstration of power and authority. The music becomes more straightforwardly tonal and forceful as he turns to the guards and calls on them to be vigilant and escort the prophet-shepherd when he arrives. He reminds them that the password is 'Pasterz' ('Shepherd'), and the guards respond briskly, their separate shouts combining to make up a temporarily reassuring chord of E flat major. But even in this exchange the King's anxiety is apparent in the still audible stabbing chromatic figures from the very opening of this act, and the insidious power of the Shepherd is further revealed when Roger's prosaic, declamatory line suddenly broadens to take in lumbering dance-rhythms at mention of the Shepherd (Ex. 24).

Ex. 24

wpro-wa-dźcie Pa - ste -rza Pro - ro   -   ka!
Lead in the Shepherd Prophet!

Edrisi, whose music also seems to show traces of the Shepherd's influence in the presence of triple-time rhythms and luxuriant harmonies, finds Roger's fear incomprehensible. It is too long, he says, since Roger listened to the words of a song or sought to kiss the lips of his consort, Roksana. Mention of Roksana is tellingly associated with the highly charged sensuous string music of the prelude to the Second Act, making it abundantly clear that in a large measure Roger's fear of the Shepherd stems from jealousy of his power over Roksana. He asks Edrisi if he saw the gleam in her eyes as the shepherd sung of his god, and whether he knows what lurks in the heart of a woman. Edrisi assures him that he is master. He should not let the grey dusk of the misty night instil such fear in him. Why the strange shudder? Persistent chromatic triplets continue throughout Roger's response. He replies that his whole body seems to be taken over by the flickering stars. He cannot understand why his heart, forged from bronze, flutters because of the starlight, as if he were a child, terrified by mysterious hostile forces. He is seized by existential dread in the face of infinity, for he now realises that his power extends only as far as the reach of his sword. Beyond that he is helpless, confronted only by the silence of the stars and his own terror. The motive which had accompanied the departure of the Shepherd in the First Act (Ex. 20) returns, slightly varied, as he frets about the unknown fire which glowed in the Shepherd's eyes. Edrisi tells the King he should banish these spectral thoughts from his mind, and listen to the night. Swans are resting while lights flicker lazily in the pools. The branches of the trees scarcely stir in the breeze – there is only the quiet rolling of waves.

Distant dance-rhythms suddenly break through on tambourine, lightly accompanying arabesques on oboe and flute which incorporate one of Szymanowski's favourite quasi-oriental formulae – streams of semitones and minor thirds (Ex. 25).

Ex. 25

The jingling of the tambourine, which seems to come from the harem, startles Roger. He mistakenly, but revealingly, imagines that it signals the arrival of the Shepherd, but after a moment of silence, the voice of Roksana can be heard offstage.

Roksana's song is the second extended solo of the opera, and is one of the few sections of the score where the melody is carried almost entirely by the voice rather than the orchestra. It is probably the best-known part of the work, but in spite of its frequent performance as a self-contained item (sometimes in the arrangement for violin and piano by Paweł Kochański[8]), it is both effective in context and indeed securely integrated within the scheme as a whole. Indeed, it provides material for a short development that fuses firmly with the subsequent scene, so making the song less of an end in itself rather than a beautiful, extended prelude to the hectic course of events which follows.

The song opens with an unaccompanied, wordless melisma, composed again of minor thirds and semitones (Ex. 26).

Ex. 26

It gives way to a further wordless strain, this time joined by the orchestra in counterpoint (Ex. 27).

---

[8] The transcription dates from 1926, the year of the first performance of the opera. An effective recital item, it extends the range of the original melismata and in general exploits the higher ranges of the violin.

Ex. 27

The main part of the song is almost in the nature of a lullaby, its main theme incorporating a stepwise arch figure that relates to the *Neanes* tag from the First Act (Ex. 28). In structure it is strophic, with the introductory material periodically returning as a refrain.

Ex. 28

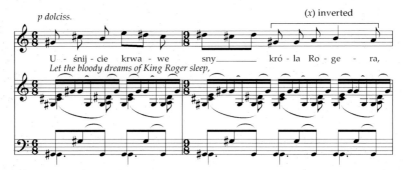

U - śnij - cie   krwa - we   sny____   kró - la   Ro - ge - ra,
Let the bloody dreams of King Roger sleep,

Women's voices join at climactic moments in each of the strophes, with additional sensuous effect. Roksana tells the King he should let his blood-thirsty anger sleep, allow the balm of the night to calm his will and let his vengeful heart be filled with mercy. He should be gracious to the Shepherd, no longer act like a tired, blood-thirsty leopard. As the song proceeds, the music moves away from the tonal region of C sharp minor to E flat major with particularly warming effect. Roksana tells the King that not even the goshawk is out hunting, but her anxiety is evident in the way part of her opening melisma is taken up by the orchestra in a series of increasingly close, tense imitations. The tonality is forced back to C sharp minor, and the music plunges into a faster tempo and increasingly dense, less tonally secure structures as Roger starts up and fearfully demands to know who it is approaching the guards. It is of course the Shepherd, as Edrisi tells him. The guards challenge the newcomer and off-stage fanfares consisting of the open fifth of F and C can be heard, preceding the Shepherd's powerful, joyous response: 'Password, Roger'.

Motifs associated with the Shepherd from the First Act can be heard played softly but persuasively in the orchestra, the ease and grace of this music contrasting markedly with the preceding moments of frenzy. Szymanowski's directions at this point call for a prolonged silence. As the music resumes, movement behind the doors is sensed, and even affects the guards. The gates swing open and the Shepherd can now be seen with four companions. Behind him soldiers swarm around, some holding torches. The Shepherd is dressed in Indian style, bedecked with many jewels. From underneath his turban, dark copper locks of hair fall onto his shoulders. His companions are similarly attired, if less richly so. For a moment, the Shepherd looks round the courtyard, before advancing in a free, spirited manner towards the King. His companions, walking several steps behind him, are carrying oriental musical instruments, and seat themselves with mysterious composure on carpets, remaining motionless for the time being. The gates slam shut and the Shepherd takes up a position on the right of the stage, confronting the King. Throughout this passage, various motifs are brought together in a gradual crescendo, some clearly related to the Shepherd's earlier music, others more explicitly dance-like in rhythm. The initially unstable harmonic structures begin to take on a whole-tone colouring, and are eventually grounded on a pedal D as the theme of the Shepherd's song from the First Act sweeps in high up on the strings, eventually climaxing with a colossal, tonally unambiguous statement of the opening of the song in A Lydian over open fifths of A and E.

The music makes it clear from the opening of this scene that it is the Shepherd who holds the upper hand. He greets Roger in the name of great love. Roger immediately attempts to assert his authority. He demands to know where the Shepherd has come from, and here the motifs which had earlier accompanied the entry of the king and consort in the First Act are again heard, but now with strangely incongruous effect. And as if to underline the already crumbling regal persona, the stabbing chromatic motif from the very opening of the Second Act reappears, plunging down to new depths of fear and despair. To the accompaniment of sweetly delicate music, featuring solo strings, celeste and various tremolo effects, the Shepherd replies that he has come from the smile of southern stars, and has prayed for Roger by the banks of the Benares and offered further prayers by the Ganges. Roger is at first puzzled, then exasperated. In reply to questions about the origins of the Shepherd's dubious powers, the King is directed to ask the silent trees at noontide, roses basking in the heat of the sun and the sweet nectar of the vineyards. From this point onwards, a motif which had been discernible at the moment the Shepherd entered now becomes increasingly prominent (Ex. 29). In various forms it runs throughout the series of exchanges which follow, its arch-like shape subjected to a number of ingenious permutations that provide a unifying framework.

Ex. 29

Roger demands to know who sent the Shepherd. 'God!' comes the reply, and here the opening of the Shepherd's song from the First Act blazes out again, now in D Lydian. He was summoned from the green estates of Paradise, plucked like a blossom from the flowers of the meadows, from peach orchards when almond blossom gives off its sweet fragrance. Rushing figures, trills and whole-tone harmonies combine with thrilling effect as he tells of how he came into being, as if like myrrh on a burnt offering, rising from the waves like the rays of the sun. He was born as if like the wings of white birds from the womb of the blue sea. Here the ecstatic culmination of his song, sweeping, soaring lines in the woodwinds, harmonised in stringent fourths chords, combine with a deep, sonorous bass.

The Shepherd's weird exultancy and spectacular blasphemies terrify Roger, who falls back dismayed, not knowing how best to counter him. Power begins to leach away from the King as the interior of the courtyard is filled, little by little, by crowds of people, beautiful young women, youths, eunuchs and boys who slip in through the many doors, run down the steps, crowd in at the doors and windows to form a wide semi-circle at the back of the stage. The Shepherd's mysterious power is again evident, for all eyes are fixed on him and the arms of the women reach out towards him in longing. Excitement and anticipation can be sensed in everyone, and once again, Roksana is heard offstage, exhorting the King to cast aside his fear and anger. Though her melody draws on previous motifs, there is a marked sense of anxiety, for her song is provided with taut harmonic structures, while the theme itself rises imploringly, ever higher. The Shepherd turns first in the direction of the still invisible Roksana, and then back to Roger. Does the King hear her plaintive song, floating towards them like the sound of a nightingale? In an unknown heart, love blossoms like a flower in the night. In drawing attention to the connection which seems to exist between himself and the King's consort, underlined by the linking of motives associated with each of them, the shepherd certainly does nothing to soothe the King, and the argument now proceeds with increased vehemence. The Shepherd reminds Roger that it was he who wanted the trial to take place, but Roger realises that the Shepherd can elude capture, like a winged bird or silver-scaled serpent. The poisonous glow of distant, alien stars glows in his eyes. Here the whole-tone harmony which opened the Second

Act reappears and moves around in a trembling organum, underlaid by weirdly accelerating, distant thuds on timpani. Roger ignores Roksana's increasingly anxious pleas on behalf of the Shepherd, and demands to know what sorcery he uses to fetter this crowd of madmen and slaves who blindly follow him. What do they believe in? He is told the people believe in the Shepherd himself, and again a luxuriant version of his song can be heard in the orchestra. For the first time since the start of the trial, Edrisi intervenes, attempting to calm the King, but the Shepherd goes on to state, unhelpfully, that they all believe in the light of his eyes, his smile and his dance-song. Roger has had enough. The Shepherd is no prophet, but rather one whose mysterious powers are drawn from the depths of hell. He is clearly intent on leading the crowd around them into the abyss of death.

The Shepherd retorts that on the contrary he enkindles passions from the depths of life. The music changes markedly in character here (*poco vivace ma con dolcezza e tranquillo*), the Shepherd's gently oscillating line, drawn from motifs from the First Act, accompanied by *sul tasto* trills on strings, with underlying pedal, rippling piano figurations and soft dance-rhythms on timpani. He points to the people clustering round him, like a swarm of coloured butterflies round sweet-scented scarlet roses. They revolve around him, hanging on the radiance from his eyes. The tempo picks up again (*Vivace poco agitato*), as he calls on the young men and maidens, bidding them take flight on wings of frenzy. An ostinato, a forceful, rapid duple-time figure, cuts through the texture as he calls on his companions to start their dance-song, with its silver bells and tambourine rhythms. The King will now see how secret desires well up in convulsive waves from the depths of the heart.

The ostinato breaks off and the musicians tune up – a wonderfully irrational sound concocted from flutter-tongued chromatic scales on flute, an intermittent four-note figure on oboe, a monotone rhythm on trumpet, quiet cymbal roll and triangle, celesta figurations, harp *glissandi*, string harmonics and muted trills. Its function is not merely picturesque, but rather like the opening of the First Violin Concerto, a signal that the listener is being transported onto a different plane, preparing the way for a powerful manifestation of Dionysian forces. This episode, far from being a self-indulgent piece of ballet, shoehorned into the scheme of things as so often happened in nineteenth-century opera, is a dramatic necessity that marks a decisive new stage in the conflict between the King and the Shepherd.

It is significant that the Shepherd refers specifically to a dance-song, the title also conferred on two passages from *Also sprach Zarathustra* where Nietzsche's hero addresses himself to the life he feels within himself. It is as yet the most direct demonstration of the Dionysian in the opera, the dance being so powerful that there is nothing in nature that is not roused to leap and run. It is, as was seen in an earlier section of this study,[9] a reaffirmation of the union, not only between man and man, but between man and nature which has become alienated, hostile or subjugated. It is that moment when, in Nietzsche's words, the barriers between man set up by 'hostile convention' are broken, that moment the veil of maya is torn aside to flutter in tatters before mysterious primordial unity. As Nietzsche put it,[10] in song and dance man feels himself a god, walking about 'enchanted, in ecstasy, like the gods he saw walking in his dreams'. Or, as D. H. Lawrence expressed it in *The Plumed Serpent*, written within the same decade as Szymanowski's opera, to join the dance is 'to be merged in desire, beyond desire, to be gone in the body beyond the individualism of the body'.[11]

It is this very abandonment in a body beyond the individualism of the body that is apparent as the crowd in the courtyard begin to spin around under the charm of the music. Roger watches in mute horror as the dance becomes increasingly abandoned. The shepherd gazes into Roger's face with a mysterious smile. The power of the music results from its hypnotic $\frac{7}{8}$ (4 + 3) rhythms, and from the accumulation of tension by way of a gradual crescendo and acceleration. The seemingly oriental oboe melody which appears over the opening bitonal ostinato (Ex. 30) sounds so authentic that the composer was quizzed about its source by the musicologist Zdzisław Jachimecki:

> Concerning the theme of the dance, about which you ask, it is absolutely my patent. I am delighted that I so succeeded in counterfeiting its 'authenticity' that you felt obliged to search out truly 'authentic' sources for verification. It is my triumph over the sweet 'orientalism' of the Rimsky's *e tutti quanti*.[12]

Undoubtedly, Szymanowski intuitively recaptured the essence of Arabic music, and indeed it is not difficult to pick out the characteristic melodic units of the modern modal system, or maqāmat, an extensive body of scales which, unlike the scales and modes of European art music, are frequently microtonal. Roksana's song, earlier in the Second Act, had drawn heavily on the combination of semitone and augmented second. Though something of a nineteenth-century 'oriental' cliché, this figure can be traced back to such chromatic units as the *sipahr* and *nagrīz* ajnas, the characteristic formulae which were used to build more extended scales. In the case of the dance-

---

[9] *Cf.* p. 90, above.

[10] Friedrich Nietzsche, *The Birth of Tragedy*, translated by W. Kaufmann, Vintage, New York, 1967, p. 37.

[11] D. H. Lawrence, *The Plumed Serpent*, Penguin, Harmondsworth, 1950, p. 141

[12] Letter to Zdzisław Jachimecki, dated 26 April 1927, in *Karol Szymanowski Korespondencja*, Vol. 3, *op. cit.*, p. 101.

song (and incidentally some of the *Songs of the Infatuated Muezzin* of 1918), the closest unit is the *sabā* ajna (Ex. 31).

Ex. 30

Ex. 31

The melodic element proved to be the one which Szymanowski stylised most obviously. Certainly, he made no attempt to incorporate the intricate rhythmic procedures of Arabic music, but there is a colouristic differentiation of accents which corresponds with the distinction made by Arab musicians when it comes to sonorities on rhythm instruments. In other words, it is possible to discern a 'dark' strong beat (the *dum*) and a contrasting 'light' beat (the *tak*). Besides these, there are five secondary sonorities and the colouring of each beat helps define the metre. Here the *dum* is based on F (double-bass, cellos, second harp, clarinet and timpani, reinforced by cymbal and bass drum) and the *taks* occur on second, fourth and sixth quavers (*pizzicato* second violins, piano, first harp and tambour basque). The *taks* are also differentiated harmonically, producing three distinct qualities of sound; the intermediate beats (third and fifth quavers) are remarkably 'unstressed', given their significance in a purely European context, although the third quaver is strengthened by being dotted. The final and weakest quaver of the bar is sustained over the barline by the second bassoon. The comparative absence of dynamic stress in favour of colour results in one of Szymanowski's most imaginative orchestrations, and it contributes strongly to the hypnotic, timeless feel to the music. This quality recedes only when Szymanowski abandons stylised, 'coloured' rhythms for a more dynamic, 'Dionysian' and essentially European pulse.

The opening of the dance is deceptively relaxed (*moderato*): the sinuous oboe line intertwines with fragments of itself on flute and clarinet and seems to be without beginning or end. Eventually it is joined by strings playing in intoxicating parallel sixths. The first rise in tension comes with a change of time signature to $\frac{3}{4}$ and a slight acceleration in pace. A new motif appears, characterised by a repeated-note figure (Ex. 32) which constantly reappears, slightly varied.

Ex. 32

The dance begins to take flight with another change of signature (to $\frac{6}{8}$) and a further additional theme (*più vivace, poco agitato*) on flute (Ex. 33).

Ex. 33

The opening phrase of the dance is heard rhythmically augmented on horns and is taken up on high strings, dying away in quiet, restrained ecstasy at the end of this first main span of the dance.

Women's voices are now heard, and the dance is resumed more urgently with a further change of signature and pace ($\frac{3}{8}$: *molto vivace, ansioso*). The anxious chromatic motives from the first part of the act are heard as

Roksana herself is seen in the upper gallery. She runs down the steps in excitement, leading Roger to start from his seat, his sudden movement conveyed by a distortion of the melisma that had opened Roksana's aria earlier in the act. He signals that she should stay where she is, but the dance continues unabated, and the Shepherd turns slowly towards Roksana, the pair of them gazing intently at each other. Roger flings himself back on the throne and buries his face in his hands. Roksana somewhat diffidently begins to sing, and the Shepherd joins with her. For an instant the music becomes less harmonically ambiguous and the wildly gyrating movements in the orchestral parts widen in ambitus. The men also join the women in song, and as the Shepherd and Roksana sing together, their language seems to fall apart in their attempts to express the ecstasy which can only be conveyed through music and the dance. 'A blazing dawn', sings Roksana, demanding to be led into the Shepherd's 'distant beyond'. The Shepherd is even less coherent: 'In a dance of love with fire in the blood to everlasting passion! In a paradise of bliss! In a heavenly dance of secret abandon!' There is a brief halt to the dance as Roger calls out to Roksana 'in the deepest distress'. The music resumes its headlong rush, with new widely oscillating motives, and further scarcely coherent utterances from both Roksana and the Shepherd: 'Cold, gardens, dance, passions, wings to fly'. The chorus whoop joyously as Roksana's line swings around with wild abandon (Ex. 34).

Roger can stand it no longer, and in a vicious *parlando*, underlaid with a savage, dislocated orchestral texture, orders the guards to seize and bind the Shepherd. An awe-inspiring cacophony accompanies his attempt to shackle the messenger of Dionysus, in effect a disastrously misdirected bid to suppress vital life-forces. The only clearly identifiable motives to emerge are those associated with Roger's own fear and anxiety (Ex. 35).

The dancing immediately subsides, leaving the people inexpressibly distressed. The guards bind the Shepherd's hands with chains, but he breaks free of them, and stands on the steps near Roksana. With fury he addresses the court. Who dares to bind him with slaves' fetters? The whole-tone structure which had run through much of the opening music of the act is carried over from the preceding uproar, and supports weak, attenuated variants of the motif relating to Roger's agony and inner battle. A shortened version of the music representing the binding of the Shepherd is heard as he tears off his chains and flings them at Roger's feet.

The Shepherd appeals with a new power and intensity directly to the people. He commands them to look on his freed arms, and all those who are free should follow him to his distant far-away land (Ex. 36).

Ex. 34

Ex. 35

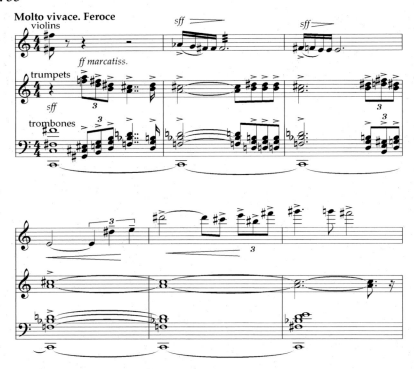

Ex. 36

O, spójrz-ciegłę-bią serc__ na wol - ne me__ ra - mio - na,
O, from the depths of your heart look at my freed arms,

He will draw his followers along paths of joy into his own kingdom, into the sweet shade of olive groves, to his world of murmuring brooks, triumphant shouts and the dance of divine maidens. In response to this call to the mysterious far-away land, Roksana and the people again take up an increasingly energetic strain as, mesmerised, they repeat his words. The Shepherd urges them to listen to the stillness of the night and the sea bearing the distant call. Who will follow him? He looks determinedly at Roger, but meets with no reply. He moves towards the doors, accompanied by the same music (Ex. 17[13]) which had marked his exit in the First Act. Roksana follows as if in a trance, and gradually various members of the court join her. Roger suddenly rouses himself, and demands to be told where he is leading the people. He receives no direct answer to his question, only that if he wishes really to judge the Shepherd, he must follow him to his sunny shores. Does he understand?

The harmonic pace picks up as motives from the dance recur, expanding in melodic range and overlapping with themselves. A massive crescendo leads back to a reprise of the final part of the dance, the people again whooping ecstatically, as Roksana's line swings around a central point accompanied by layers of *ostinati*. The shepherd can be heard, again calling on Roger to heed his words, as the people rush off. Their rapid, wing-like flight into the distance is conveyed by a skilfully contrived Doppler effect, their fading, falling lines outlining the note sequence B flat, A, F sharp and F, in other words a part of the characteristic figure of Roksana's melisma (Ex. 26[14]). The stage is left deserted, save for Roger, his head in his hands, and Edrisi, watching his master with considerable anxiety. The troubled whole-tone motif of the opening music of the Second Act returns as the King utters Roksana's name. Edrisi stares through the window into the darkness. Night has enveloped the entire crowd, and the sound of their voices and tramp of feet is dying away. Ghostly echoes of motives from the dance can be heard. So too can reminiscences of the King's agony. Suddenly, this motive develops into a whirlwind of sound (*Vivace e agitato*) as Roger, after a moment's thought, takes off his crown and mantle, and throws his

---

[13] *Cf.* p. 107, above.
[14] *Cf.* p. 112, above.

sword rattling to the ground. He will follow in the tracks of the crowd. He will go as a pilgrim. A bleak, very soft open fifth on trombones can be heard as the curtain falls.

Act Three

The final act is set in the ruins of an ancient Greek theatre, the place of the original manifestation of the Dionysian in art. Stone benches curve in a semi-circle from the front, right, to the rear of the stage, reaching almost half the height of the stage. Above them there is the infinity of the sky. The theatre is in a state of ill repair, the stone polished and weathered by its exposure to the elements for hundreds of years. Weeds and wild flowers grow from cracks and crevices, and there is a covering of grass over some parts of the stage. Everywhere there is evidence of decay and neglect. The ruined stage extends obliquely up to the left, its shattered columns still standing, though the ornate capitals, friezes and metopes which once decorated the theatre are scattered around. The remains of statues can be seen on pedestals, though their heads, arms and torsos also lie on the ground. An almost intact double staircase leads on to the stage, and the remains of a wall behind the stage have also survived. The remains of an altar are visible. It seems that a sacrifice has recently been made to an 'unknown god', for plumes of smoke still rise from it, and garlands and flowers have been left at its base. At the back of the stage, there is an enormous gap between the ancient stage and the rows of seats, and through it the limitless expanse of the sea can be detected. Stars shine brightly, and a pale moon casts a faint light over the interior of the ruins, casting long shadows and emphasising the blackness of the gaps in the walls. Everything is still, apart from the sea, tireless and restless, pounding heavily on the rocky shore.

The music preceding the King's entry is desolate and bleak, and is characterised by a new bareness and astringency, pointing to a stripping-away of inessentials, a laying-bare of the soul. Indeed, what is witnessed here is Roger's night-journey of the soul, a harrowing and lonely experience tellingly characterised in the lean two-part string-writing. It eventually combines with a further line on clarinet, the dotted rhythms of which convey a faint trace the exultation of the preceding act (Ex. 37).

Roger and Edrisi enter stage right. The king is dressed in a shabby, dust-covered tunic, his hair dishevelled. He is weary, and sits on one of the stones, burying his head in his hands. After a moment he looks around, but sees nothing but lifeless stones, the boundless ocean and the mysterious silvery starlight. Another bleak motive emerges (Ex. 38 (a)), which coincidentally anticipates the opening of Szymanowski's *Stabat Mater* of 1925–26, where it is used to depict a scene of the utmost desolation (Ex. 38 (b)).

Ex. 37

Ex. 38

(a)

(b)

Stabat Mater, bars 1-2

Roger asks Edrisi where he has brought him. Is this ruin to be the end of their wanderings? Here, amidst stones, with the ghastly spectre of exhausted ecstasy keeping watch? The austere opening motives are joined by a yearning, grief-laden line for horn, rising only to fall again helplessly (Ex. 39).

Ex. 39

Roger fears that any attempt to summon other presences in the theatre will only be answered by bewitched laughter. Here a weirdly attenuated distortion of Roksana's melismatic line is heard, leading Edrisi to urge the King to call and waken the echoes of the ruins (Ex. 40).

Ex. 40

For the moment the King ignores him, pursuing his own disturbed train of thought. He is tired; the coming dawn is lulling him to sleep like a child. Where has his beloved Roksana gone? He has become a tramp, a whining beggar, begging charity and hiding his empty heart in worn-out tatters of dreams. His recognition of his own spiritual hollowness is underlined by a return of the opening motives. Hate and love are empty words. Might and authority are consumed by flames. Who is it he is seeking? Whose song does he crave? A faint reminiscence of one of the motives associated with the Shepherd provides an answer of sorts. Edrisi again urges Roger to call for Roksana. His advice meets with a frightened, irrational response. For Roger, fear lies dormant in the void, and a pageant of spectres drifts by dancing. Should he rouse the phantoms? Should he conjure up dreams? His terror is conveyed by largely chromatic, non-thematic flashes of sound, which give way to nervous, jagged references to the opening theme of the Third Act. He composes himself, and calls Roksana's name. A low pedal C (double-bass tremolo) and very soft strokes on timpani seem to indicate the awakening of the ghosts of the amphitheatre. He calls again, and this time is answered by Roksana.

Edrisi stands amazed. Witchery has been awakened. It seems to Roger that the voice comes from over the sea. Emboldened, he calls again, but this time it is the Shepherd who replies. 'Hate! Love! Will there be no end to doubt?' asks the king. Off-stage voices can be heard, a wordless incantation of motives from the dance in the Second Act, with solo soprano and tenor voices greeting the King who has shattered his sword and come to stand trial (Ex. 41).

They are accompanied by pedal C and rippling clarinet figures and increasingly luxuriant sounds (flutter-tongued flute, string harmonics, harp *glissandi* and piano *tremolandi*). Roksana can again be heard, now coming gradually closer, singing of a heart burning like a torch ready for sacrifice to God. The King remains fearful, but the Shepherd, still out of sight, attempts to reassure him, telling him to leave his fear behind, along with his broken sword. The moon suddenly emerges from behind the clouds, bathing the ruins in a mysterious light. Roger looks around in quiet wonder, the music (*molto tranquillo*) depicting the fantastical unreality of the scene, the underlying scarcely marked pulse a slow, floating duple time, with familiar motives drifting together. Edrisi, too, marvels at the ghostly light and silvery magic that seems to be summoning up false dreams. Roksana appears, and Roger looks at her feverishly. Is it really her? He recognises her red lips, her same sweet smile, the same bright golden hair. But in her eyes there shines a secret deeper than the brilliance of the stars. Is it really Roksana, or only a pallid apparition born of foolish longing? In response to Roger's troubled outburst, Roksana sweetly sings that she really is there, that she is coming to him at daybreak, that she will take him by the arm, lead him through the gates of her palace. There he can rest on her bed. The C sharp pedal which had supported the closing stages of Roger's outburst continues to sound, but in place of the troubled chromaticised versions of earlier themes, radiant sonorities and a modally tinged major-key melody can now be heard (Ex. 42).

Roger wants to know where the Shepherd is. Roksana tells him he has gone, disappeared, melted away in the mist. In the distance there is, as Szymanowski's stage-directions say, 'strange music, like plaintive female voices and pan-pipes'. Roksana explains that it is only the faint singing of flutes, like the sobbing of a distant echo. Roger is not convinced. He has picked out the distant call of the Shepherd, and again demands to know where he is.

Ex. 41

Ex. 42

(As if in a dream)

Jes - tem przy to - bie, Kró - lu Pa - nie! I - dę do cie - bie
I am with you, O King! I come to you at daybreak! Give me your hand, Roger!

wran-nym świ - ta - niu! Daj mi swą rę - kę, Ro - ge - rze!__

He is told that the Shepherd is in the stars, in thunder-storms, and hovers like a golden spirit around the fire that smoulders on the altar, the smoke from which ascends to the heavens. As Roksana struggles to express her idea of the Shepherd's omnipresence, vague references to motives associated with the Shepherd's power can be distinguished. She points to the stage and tells the King that eternal longing dwells there, at the centre of the ruins; it is from that very spot that he calls to the depths of Roger's heart, wanting to make his solitary power eternal. The Shepherd again calls Roger, and Roksana urges him to make a burnt offering. They hasten to the altar, Roger demanding that they save the sparks from the ashes, a poignant image for his own spiritual state and approaching phoenix-like rebirth. A hugely imposing, widely spanning falling bass line culminates in a mighty obliterating sound involving heavy percussion as they throw flowers and garlands at the foot of the altar onto the remains of the fire which bursts into flames. At that moment, the Shepherd in the form of Dionysus appears in the ruins. There is, according to the stage-directions, something unearthly about the scene. Brilliance radiates from the Shepherd, as if he were the source of the light; everything around is thrown into deeper darkness. The presence of numerous figures which are about to appear more clearly in the amphitheatre is sensed rather than seen. As the next scene progresses, the sound of flutes and human voices grows in intensity.

Roger's trial has begun, a trial by sweet and insidious ordeal in which he must fight to withstand the temptation to remain in the Shepherd's land, the region of the 'far-away', with its primitive, undifferentiated consciousness. It is only through enduring such a trial that Roger can hope to emerge as a fully integrated being. Once again, the Shepherd summons Roger. Does the king hear his voice which in the depths of his own heart sings eternally a song of joy? Throughout this scene, the vocal parts are supported by a C pedal with chromatic chordal *tremolandi* (Ex. 43).

Ex. 43

Ro-ge - rze!   Ro-ge - rze!   Czy sły-szysz głos mój?
Roger! Roger! Do you hear my voice? Which in the depths of your heart sings

Cowie czy-ście   zglę bin twe-go ser - ca   śpie-wa pieśń ra - do   -   sną?
eternally a song of joy?

The Shepherd's line, with its repeated descents and chromatic inflections, inspires the people, still out of sight, to call on Roger to listen to the message. The Shepherd's song gradually rises in tessitura as he tells of the flames blazing up to the heavens, of divine radiance and joyous ecstasy. The people join in the song, their music a quietly joyous variation of one of the dance-themes, with the Shepherd's incantatory line modified to take in a diatonicised variant of the opening descending motive (Ex. 44.)

Ex. 44

Shepherd

U śmie-cha się   ta - jem - ni - ca,   głę-bie sta-ją się prze - rzy - ste
The mystery smiles, the depths become transparent.

Off-stage chorus

Czy   sły - szysz zew,   ta - jem   -   ny   zew?__
Do you hear the call, the mysterious call?

The mystery is smiling, the depths become transparent. In the depths of the King's lonely heart is his never before dreamed dream of endless power! Throughout, the King stands transfixed, staring feverishly at the ghostly figure of the Shepherd with his arms outstretched. Dawn begins to break, and the stars slowly fade. Woodwinds join the voices as they shout to Roger, their cries and exclamations intensifying with every moment. These siren-like birdcalls come to form part of an orchestral texture in which every part dances, oscillating in abandon. The pedal C, now reinforced by organ, supports dense harmonic structures which rise first through the tonal regions of D, E, F and A flat to heady effect. The Shepherd calls on the people to follow him to the blue sea, the boundless ocean, to join in the infinite wandering of the joyous dance.

Roksana joins in, her line swooping and soaring as she sings of the transport of the song, the transport of the dance, the call to a land of ecstasy. The particularly dense texture here incorporates myriads of melodic fragments, some reminiscent of material from other middle-period works,[15] as if Szymanowski were throwing the whole of his musical vocabulary behind the Shepherd's appeal. The tonal region rises again, first to B flat and then, at the climax of the scene, to D flat. At this moment, marked by the maximum intensity of movement both in the music and on stage, Roksana, in whom a mysterious power has been perceived, throws off her long cloak and reveals herself in the form of a Greek maenad, a frenzied follower of Dionysus. Crowds of figures can be seen in the uncertain dawn light, emerging at the top of the amphitheatre. They rush down the steps to the centre of the stage, encircling the Shepherd. The light emanating from the Shepherd grows dimmer, and he finally vanishes from view. In the meantime, Roksana seizes a thyrsus, the Bacchantes' staff wreathed in ivy or vine leaves, and runs towards the stage, vanishing in the crowd milling around. Roger seems not to be aware of what is going on, as if he is plunged in a trance.

As the shouting dies down, the various dance-motives begin to steady themselves, and the ostinati which had run through the preceding passage begin to fall apart rhythmically. The texture thins out until, as the crowd disperses completely and the flames on the altar flicker out, the desolate themes of the opening of the act return. Now, by contrast, these motifs are not allowed to develop again. After the unearthly light of the Dionysian revelation comes the rising sun, primordial symbol of rebirth and recovery from the perils of the soul. The morning light intensifies. The first copper-golden rays of the sun shine across the top of the theatre, leaving the interior itself in comparative darkness. Edrisi seems to come to his senses: the dream is over and the chains of illusion broken. Roger looks around joyfully. As if drawn by a mysterious force, he makes his way to the back of the stage. Here there is music new in both substance and mood, far removed from the desolation of the opening and the exultancy of the Dionysia. Now there is only peace, calm, deep joy and radiance as the sun-light gains in strength (Ex. 45), a horn motif heard against a static whole-tone background.

Hesitantly at first, then more insistently, as an energetic rising and falling motive makes its appearance, Roger makes his way to the top of the theatre, watched by an amazed Edrisi. Bathed in brilliant sun-light, he sings a hymn

---

[15] For example, *Métopes*, Op. 29, and the First Violin Concerto, Op. 35.

to the rising sun, and for the first and only time in the opera, his music begins to approach the lyrical as he surveys the scene before him. Not only the sun, but sails like the white wings of gulls, unfurled on the blue depths of the sea. They sail into infinity, lightly and nimbly, like the white foam of the waves. The wings expand. They look set to take over the whole world. His recognition and integration of the Dionysian is conveyed by faint dance-rhythms and lines which embrace in both diatonic and chromatic form the three-note cell which had characterised Roksana's music as well as a falling motive from the Shepherd's incantation (Ex. 46).

Ex. 45

Ex. 46

At this vision of the wings embracing the world, the music climaxes on a chord of D major, underpinned by another pedal C. This pedal, which had underlaid the whole of the Dionysian revelation, is sustained to the close of the work. As the embodiment of a new modern awareness that differentiates him from 'the all-embracing, pristine unconsciousness which claims the bulk of mankind almost entirely',[16] Roger is left on his own. Yet from the depths of solitude, from the abyss of his power, he tears out his transparent heart and gives it in offering to the sun. As the curtain falls, and accompanied by a massive C major chord, Roger stretches out his cupped hands to the golden sun, as if bearing a priceless gift.

[16] C. G. Jung, *Modern Man in Search of a Soul*, Routledge, London, 1933, p. 227.

VI
Performance History:
A Brief Survey

The first of the three productions of *King Roger* staged during Szymanowski's lifetime was mounted in Warsaw at the Teatr Wielki ('Grand Theatre'). The premiere was repeatedly delayed, in part because of instability following a *coup d'état* by General Piłsudski on 12–14 May 1926,[1] but it eventually took place on 19 June 1926. The conductor was Emil Młynarski,[2] and the principal roles were taken by Eugeniusz Mossakowski (Roger), the composer's sister, Stanisława Korwin-Szymanowska (Roksana), Adam Dobosz (the Shepherd), Maurycy Janowski (Edrisi), Teodozja Skoniezcna (the Deaconess) and Roman Wraga (the Archiereios).

The work posed considerable difficulties in rehearsal. Ilza Rodzińska (wife of the conductor Artur Rodziński) was appointed *répétiteur* as all other staff pianists avoided the undertaking. Writing several decades later, she described the preparation of *King Roger* as 'the most burdensome musical task of my career'.[3] Basic training of the soloists took around four months before they were ready for rehearsals with the orchestra. In fact, the role of Roksana was allotted to Stanisława Szymanowska only after two other singers had resigned the part. Mossakowski found memorisation of the part challenging, and Dobosz was initially unable to hold his part against the sometimes complex accompaniment. As a consequence, Rodzińska had to simplify the piano reduction, and then gradually build up the texture. Szymanowski attended rehearsals only towards the end:

> It was onerous for the singers because Karol often said in his characteristically pleasant, gentle way: 'Miss Ilza, isn't it possible to take this a little faster' [...].

[1] Following the failure of the economic-reform programme of the Skryński government, Wincenty Witos's Piast Peasant Party assumed control on 10 May. Józef Piłsudski, who had been active in the fight for Polish independence since the early years of the century, led demonstrations against the right-wing programme of the Witos administration, eventually taking control of the country after three days of fighting which left 500 dead and 1,000 wounded.

[2] Emil Młynarski (1870–1935) was conductor, composer and violinist. He was director of the Warsaw Opera and conducted the first performances of both *Hagith* and *King Roger*.

[3] Ilza Rodzińska, 'Jak przygotowywaliśmy "Króla Rogera"' ('How we prepared "King Roger"'), *Ruch Muzyczny*, 1983, No 5, p. 6, reproduced in *Karol Szymanowski Korespondencja*, Vol. 2, *op. cit.*, p. 462.

The Teatr Wielki in the early years of the twentieth century

I had to persuade him that the singers really were trying very hard and that they couldn't go any faster. When we approached the final stages, however, he was very satisfied and grateful.[4]

Indeed, he was so pleased with the results that he urged Emil Hertzka of Universal Edition to attend the premiere, writing that the work made an unusually powerful impression. At the same time, he complained that the piano reduction by Arthur Willner,[5] which he had previously approved, did not give a true impression of the essence of the music, but instead implied the presence of huge, unheard-of difficulties which in reality did not exist: 'naturally it is not *Traviata*, but it is much easier than *Elektra*'.[6] To Zofia Kochańska he remarked that a superficial reading of the piano reduction

---

[4] *Ibid.*, p. 462.

[5] The Czech-born Willner (1881–1959) was commissioned by Universal Edition to produce the reduction as Szymanowski did not wish to undertake the task. An important composer and teacher in his own right, the Jewish Willner fled from Vienna to Paris immediately after the *Anschluss*, settling in Britain later in 1938. His own substantial output of compositions (which includes six string quartets) has fallen into near-complete oblivion.

[6] Letter dated 31 May 1926, in *ibid.*, II, p. 458.

*Emil Młynarski, who conducted
the first performance of* King Roger

('which is terrible') could not substitute for experiencing the music in full: 'I must confess that in performance with orchestra and chorus it creates in places a simply *amazing* effect.'[7]

The production adhered closely to Szymanowski's requirements of the staging, and there were many enthusiastic comments from the critics about the singers. Mossakowski was praised for his delivery of Szymanowski's 'exceedingly difficult musical phrases' which were 'given so beautifully that it was possible to regard them as the last word in musical expression.'[8] Dobosz was highly commended for his phenomenal musicality, his performance of the Shepherd 'charming with sounds of beauty and love,'[9] and, in the words of the same reviewer, Stanisława was 'completely consumed in the sacrificial devotion of her splendid vocal art to the service of the beloved work of her brother.'[10] There was praise, too, for the orchestra and conductor, as well as the choir and their chorus-master, Dagobert Polzinetti, and the direction, under the control of Mieczysław Popławski, was described as being 'beyond

[7] Letter dated 5 June 1926, in *ibid.*, II, p. 461.
[8] Władysław Fabry, '"Król Roger" Karola Szymanowskiego' ('"King Roger" of Karol Szymanowski') *Polska Zbrojna* ('Armed Poland'), 1926, No. 169, p. 6, in *ibid.*, II, p. 478.
[9] *Ibid.*, p. 478.
[10] *Ibid.*, p. 478.

reproach'. Sets and costumes, although borrowed in some cases from earlier productions, as well as the choreography were also 'beyond reproach'.[11]

As regards the work itself, the tone of the reviews ranged from enthusiastic on the part of critics associated with progressive publications (Jarosław Iwaszkiewicz, Juliusz Wertheim, Władysław Fabry, Henryk Opieński and Mateusz Gliński) to hostile from those usually associated with the conservative or nationalist press (Piotr Rytel, Stanisław Niewiadomski, Juliusz Kaden-Bandrowski and Karol Stromenger). All these writers made some attempts at an evaluation of the libretto. Iwaszkiewicz, who was of course responsible for the initial draft of the work, distanced himself from the project; he modestly claimed that his work was no more than a third- or fourth-rate realisation of what Szymanowski required for his music, which in any case had been subjected to extensive revision by the composer himself:

> It is not a drama, nor an oratorio – it is rather a mysterium different from all others, modelled on nothing comparable (though perhaps echoes of *The Bacchae* by Euripides can be seen here and there.[12]

For Fabry, the theme of the opera was the struggle of the soul with the material world, 'an internal battle played out in the soul of King Roger'.[13] Wertheim believed it represented the 'victorious struggle of pagan-Greek joy of life over Christian ecstasy',[14] an interpretation shared by Opieński – 'a victory of the Dionysian concept of life over [...] the Byzantine religious rigours of the King, his wife, his court and ultimately all his people'. It was – in spite of its oratorical character – a musico-poetic whole, a thoroughly theatrical creation:

> in spite of the seeming inertia of external action, the internal action has so strong a tension and intensification that it holds the listener from beginning to end.[15]

Szymanowski himself was irritated by the general tenor of some of these reviews, in particular their misrepresentations of the ideology of the work, and started to draft a reply for publication in the press. Unfortunately, he abandoned the project, but not before rejecting the identification of

---

[11] *Ibid.*, p. 478.

[12] Jarosław Iwaszkiewicz, 'Przed premierą "Króla Rogera"' ('Before the Premiere of "King Roger"'), *Wiadomości Literackie* ('Literary News'), 1926, No. 25, in *ibid.*, II, p. 470.

[13] Władysław Fabry, *loc. cit.*, p. 6, quoted in *ibid.*, II, p. 477.

[14] Juliusz Wertheim, 'Król Roger' ('King Roger'), *Nowy Kurier Polski*, 28 June 1926, quoted in *ibid.*, II, p. 471.

[15] Henryk Opieński. 'Król Roger', *Przegląd Muzyczny* ('Musical Review'), Poznań, 1926, No. 7, pp. 10–12, reprinted in *ibid.*, II, pp. 471–72.

Act 1 of King Roger *in the premiere production, Warsaw, 1926*

medieval superstition and cruelty with the Christian idea on the one hand, and the Hellenic spirit with cheap hedonism on the other, as well as the 'boundlessly naïve idea of a victorious paganism'.[16]

Other critics dismissed the underlying proposition outright. Writing in *Świat* ('World'), Kaden-Bandrowski commented that Szymanowski's huge talent had been devoted to an operatic project so remote and unreal that in the end it became a matter of indifference to the spectator:

> King Roger, Roksana, the Shepherd, the central figures of the opera, are not living people from an earlier age or period, nor are they figures from fairy stories, but rather, if we may so express it, programmes of an unclear tendency and so misty that they are incapable of creating conflict, let alone action. The figures of the opera in their continual discussions and deliberations move around the stage, failing to permit the development of a dramatic operatic scheme.[17]

Kaden-Bandrowski urged the composer to forget about his Jewish and Sicilian Kings, and take to heart 'our poor, but so rich urban life, […] our grey civilised man, without bells, weapons and swords'.[18]

Similar criticisms were levelled at the work following its next production, which took place in the Stadttheater in Duisburg (North Rhine-Westphalia)

[16] Karol Szymanowski, 'W obronie ideologii "Króla Rogera"' ('In Defence of the Ideology of "King Roger"'), in *Karol Szymanowski Pisma*, Vol. 1, *op. cit.*, p. 493.

[17] Juliusz Kaden-Bandrowski, 'Król Roger', *Świat* ('World'), 28 June 1926, quoted in *ibid.*, II, p. 472.

[18] *Ibid.*, p. 473.

on 28 October 1928. Szymanowski was scarcely involved with this production, merely stating that he favoured the German pronunciation of 'Roger' (i.e., hard rather than soft 'g'). He declined an invitation from the Intendant of the opera house, Dr Saladin Schmitt, to attend rehearsals, stressing that the performers should enjoy maximum freedom in their preparation:

> the role of the composer ceases properly at the moment when he writes the last note of the score. The same applies to the director and designer, and this is all the more important in the case of *King Roger* as an atmosphere of historic pedantry lingers in the description of the scenic aspects. For me, this pedantry counts for absolutely nothing, since my work has room for the most far-reaching fantasy.[19]

In the end, the Duisburg production realised the original concept closely, as illustrations of the sets by Johannes Schröder, reproduced in a lavish booklet prepared by the opera-house, reveal. The conductor was Paul Drach, the director Alexander Schum and the principals Holger Börgesen (Roger), Hildegard Bieber-Naumann (Roksana), Alexander Gillmann (the Shepherd) and Leonhard Kistemann (Edrisi). According to W. Jakobs, this was 'music without dramatic sense based on a text which is internally undramatic and so unable to afford possibilities for external action that everything is decorative'.[20] The piece acted like a narcotic, but thanks to the dazzling production, 'boredom was avoided'. Max Voigt particularly liked the first act, and commended not only the performers but also the beautiful sets, especially the mosaics in the chapel.[21] Erik Reger also praised the production, but asked what the opera had 'in common with us, in our time'.[22]

Although Szymanowski enjoyed much acclaim in Duisburg, the occasion was marred for him, not so much by the rather cool critical response, as a hostile demonstration organised by a right-wing faction. Everything started well. The production was, as he wrote to Zofia Kochańska and the dedicatee of the opera, Dorothy Jordan Robinson, 'very beautiful' and

> in certain respects, much superior to the Warsaw one. [...] After the end of the first act, there was mediocre enough applause, though not particularly poor; in any case, I was a little anxious since the first act is the most 'popular' and audiences have always like it, even in Warsaw. But after the second, I heard with astonishment and joy that the applause was very great. Well, I was

[19] Letter dated 8 October 1928, in *Karol Szymanowski Korespondencja*, Vol. 3, *op. cit.* I, p. 342.
[20] *Köln-Zeitung*, 30 October 1928, quoted in *ibid.*, I, p. 358.
[21] *Die Musik* 3 December 1928, as given in *ibid.*, I, p. 359.
[22] *Melos*, No. 11, November 1928, pp. 559–60, reprinted in *ibid.*, I, p. 360.

with Tala [Neuhaus[23]] in the theatre, and I listened for quite a long time with her, but at last I went into the wings as the applause went on continuously. But before I arrived, the audience quietened down and I was stranded as I did not arrive in time to appear before the public. I had promised to appear immediately after the curtain fell at the end of the third act. On leaving my seat at the end, I heard with joy that the applause was again even greater than after the second act. Finally, I appeared on stage with the singers, director etc., and then amidst the frenetic applause I heard whistles, shouts, the 'friendly' nature of which was not in any doubt. Stravinsky would have been delighted, but I was completely stupefied. What the devil was happening?! There is nothing that revolutionary in *Roger* to outrage the German public who have already experienced music of all types and who in any case are very well educated. The director said to me 'passen Sie nicht auf, das sind die Stahlhelm[24] (!!!) – kommen Sie nur'. I went on stage again. The public in general, enraged by these whistles, stayed in the hall and applauded all the more. The whistles redoubled. In the end it lasted 20 minutes, during which time I took at least 15 calls before the lights went on and everything calmed down. It was only the next day that I heard the background to this story. Well, organisations belonging to the 'right' (Stahlhelm etc., etc.) resolved to do this in the case of *Roger* because I am … Polish. It happened not just because *Roger* was part of the repertoire, but because it had been chosen by the management as one of six operas for the grand 'Operfestspielwoche' at Duisburg under the auspices of Allgemeiner Deutscher Tonkünstlerverein as *the only foreign work* (a great honour for me!). These organisations knew that the jury of the Tonkünstlerverein would be present to give their 'placet', so the Stahlhelm arranged this hostile demonstration to make this impossible. Fortunately, they did not succeed, and *Roger* was accepted by the jury. I know that after this, it was staged several times successfully. So – providing there are no further intrigues against me – it will hopefully be revived at the festival in June or the beginning of July […].[25]

In fact, political considerations prevailed in the end and Szymanowski's expectations were thwarted. He received an apology from the German ambassador in Warsaw, but the incident left deep scars and led him to block all thoughts of the opera from his mind. As a result, the performance mounted at the Národní Divadlo (National Theatre) in Prague on 21 October 1932 came as an utter revelation. Czech musicians had wanted to stage the work from as far back as the time of its Warsaw premiere. Otakar Ostrčil, the conductor of the Prague performance, had been present

---

[23] Natalie Neuhaus, sister of Harry Neuhaus and daughter of Gustav, Szymanowski's music-teacher in Elizavetgrad.

[24] A right-wing German nationalist organisation, opposed to the propagation of non-German culture.

[25] Letter dated 6 January 1929, in *Karol Szymanowski Korespondencja*, Vol. 3, *op. cit.*, II, pp. 19–20; emphasis in original.

*Set designs for the First (above) and Third (right) Acts in the Duisburg
production in 1928*

at the first production, and he worked enthusiastically on the project with
the director Józef Munclingr, who had trained and worked in Poland.
Munclingr translated the libretto into Czech, and did much to promote the
work before the performance, organising publication through the theatre
of material devoted to Szymanowski's music and encouraging the editor
of the national *Radio Journal* to include introductory articles on the opera.
Indeed, the performance was transmitted not only across Czechoslovakia
but also Germany, though not, much to Szymanowski's annoyance, and
the puzzlement of Czech Radio staff, to Poland, all offers of a relay being
ignored for no apparent reason. Szymanowski arrived the day before the first
performance (of four) and went straight to the theatre for the dress rehearsal
and then, in the evening, to an event mounted at the Club of the Circle of
Friends of Poland. It took the form of an illustrated talk by Munclingr on
matters to do with the direction, set-design and the translation of the text
from Polish to Czech. The next day Szymanowski gave a short talk on Czech
Radio (the surviving recording is one of only two of his voice). He spoke of
his feelings when attending the dress rehearsal the preceding day, of how he
found that all elements of the production – music, direction and set design
(by Václaw Pavlik) – surpassed his best expectations. He also praised the
soloists – Zděnek Otava (Roger), Ada Nordenová (Roksana), Vladimir Tomš

(the Shepherd) and Jaroslav Gleich (Edrisi) – and finished with the hope that art, 'whose purest expression is music, speaking from soul to soul and from heart to heart, would contribute to the mutual penetration and meeting of the psyche of nations'.[26]

Szymanowski's fulsome public tributes to the performers were no mere courtesies, for a letter to Zofia Kochańska reveals the extent to which he was moved on becoming reacquainted with his own masterpiece:

> Zosieńko – believe me – you have no idea what it is like! You know that I am not pretentious and rather critically inclined towards my own music – but really it simply shook me (especially the second act). The staging was in general splendid, perhaps the first [...] which has been truly expressive. It cannot be compared with anything else in my music – alas, not even with *Harnasie* or the two new concertos,[27] in effect with nothing I've written since. It's very sad!! The very sound of the orchestra and chorus is in places completely amazing and simply gripping in its tension. But I cannot shake off the impression – and with it the sad feeling – that it is all in the past and that for a certainty I could not now write anything like it. I do not want to boast

[26] Chylińska, *Szymanowski i jego epoka*, Vol. 2, *op. cit.*, p. 533.
[27] That is, Symphony No. 4 (*Symphonie concertante*) for piano and orchestra, Op. 60 (1932), and Violin Concerto No. 2, Op. 61 (1932–33).

about the simply unheard-of ovation from the public after the 2nd and 3rd acts.[28]

Photographs of the production reveal the sets to be uncluttered, with clear lines, and that soloists and chorus were effectively placed with epic effect (according to Piotr Szalsza,[29] 400 performers were involved). For one Polish reviewer – Marian Szyjkowski of the *Kurier Warszawski* – Munclingr's staging seemed too materialistic to complement the essence of the 'mysterium':

> the massing of crowds on stage, the absence of depth on stage, the realistic designs of the costumes, the ineffectual (again too materialistic) ballet – all this deprives the work of its visionary character [...].[30]

In general, though, critical opinion was both favourable and perspicacious:

> The theatrical form of the work derives completely from its musical structure. If the music were subtracted, a philosophical poem would remain which would in itself be of interest to the reader. [...] thanks to the power of the music, regardless of the apparent scarcity of action, the spectacle holds the attention of the viewer.[31]

Other writers dwelt on the way the work related to European music in general – not only with regard to the presence of perceived German and French influences, but also to whether or not it belonged to a Polish tradition:

> we ought not to look for a national character merely in accordance with traditional Slav artistic creativity as it came down to us in the 19th century. In this sense, *King Roger* is not a Polish national opera. It does not correspond at all with the character of Polish Catholicism, nor do its internal outlines match the Polish national character. *Roger* is through and through a western work of especial merit [...].[32]

It was not until after the Second World War that *King Roger* was staged once more, first in Palermo on 22 April 1949, when it was given in Italian at the Teatro Massimo under the joint auspices of the International Society for Contemporary Music and the Sicilian Department of Tourism and Spectacle. The conductor, Mieczysław Mierzejewski, and director, Bronisław

[28] Letter dated 27 October 1932, in *Karol Szymanowski Korespondencja*, Vol. 4, *op. cit.*, I, p. 327.

[29] Piotr Szalsza, 'Karol Szymanowski w Pradze' ('Karol Szymanowski in Prague'), Akademia Muzyczna im Karola Szymanowskiego w Katowicach (Karol Szymanowski Musical Academy in Katowice), 1985, p. 127.

[30] Quoted in *ibid.*, I, p. 323.

[31] Review by Helena Holečková, in *Centralna Jewropa*, 5 December 1932, reprinted in *ibid.*, I, p. 320.

[32] Review by Hubert Doležil, in *Českém slově*, 23 October 1932, reprinted in *ibid.*, p. 320.

The Narodní Divadlo, Prague

Horowicz, were engaged to spearhead preparations in collaboration with the Italian designer Renato Gussato. His sets and costumes were notable for their simplicity and marked contrasts of colour. In the Second Act in particular, Gussato followed Szymanowski's scenic descriptions closely, and the costumes for the Third were based on figures on Greek vases. By all accounts, rehearsals did not go smoothly. The Intendant, Filippo Ernesto Raccuglia, had undertaken to translate the libretto from the German version in Universal's piano reduction, but his leisurely approach to the task meant that rehearsals with the chorus and soloists were seriously delayed, and costumes and props appeared only on the very day of the dress rehearsal. Iwaszkiewicz was present, recording his admiration of the improvisatory powers of the singers who had not been given enough time to learn their parts properly. He also commented on the spontaneous chaos of the dance in the Second Act as well as the unforgettable orchestral sound with its sweet Italian strings.[33]

The general impression amongst visiting musicians and critics was that the Italian operatic approach, in conjunction with the translation, turned *King Roger* into something approaching *verismo*, and that in spite of the

---

[33] Małgorzata Komorowska, *Szymanowski w Teatrze* ('Szymanowski in the Theatre'), Instytut Sztuki Polskiej Akademii Nauk, Warsaw, 1992, p. 177.

Act One in the 1932 production in the Narodní Divadlo, Prague

dense instrumentation, 'as if embroidered with gold', the broad result was an impressionistic sound 'without Debussyism in which there is something more Northern and sadder, as if the climate of [Szymanowski's] country cast a snowy reflection on this western impressionism!'[34] Since then, *King Roger* has been twice revived successfully in Palermo, first in 1992 and most recently in 2005, when it was given in Polish.

A further sixteen years elapsed before the next production: in November 1965, along with Moniuszko's *Halka* and *Straszny Dwór* ('The Haunted Manor') and Różycki's *Pan Twardowski*, it was included in a season of Polish operas mounted to inaugurate the re-opening of Warsaw's Teatr Wielki, finally rebuilt after its destruction in the Second World War. Both Mierzejewski and Horowicz were involved in this staging as well, and the designer on this occasion was Otto Axer. As Horowicz later remarked, the much larger stage, compared with that of the Teatro Massimo, 'permitted the monumentalisation of the whole to a more pronounced degree than was possible in Sicily'.[35]

The title role was taken by the imposing Andrzej Hiolski and, according to Ludwik Erhardt, writing in *Ruch Muzyczny*, it was 'as if the role had been written specially for him. He not only sang but acted the part'.[36] He was helped in this approach both by his rich attire, with its Byzantine references, and his mastery of economic, expressive gesture. He became the focus of attention, to such an extent that he overshadowed the remaining principals.

[34] Henriette Roget, '"Roi Roger", un opéra de Szymanowski inconnu en France' ('"King Roger", an Opera by Szymanowski Unknown in France), *Paralelle 50*, quoted in *ibid.*, p. 178.
[35] *Ibid*, pp. 178–79.
[36] Ludwik Erhardt, 'Król Roger', *Ruch muzyczny*, quoted in *ibid.*, p. 179.

As Erhardt wrote, Horowicz's monumental treatment of the work was apparent in his management of the massed crowds:

> If Roger in general is rather static, then Horowicz further intensified this static quality. On stage there is simply little movement: the soloists move rather intermittently and slowly and sparingly, and the choir is almost stationary – if they move at all it is only as a disciplined mass, angrily reacting to the shepherd, surrounding him, or withdrawing in horror at the sight of the breaking chains. The director explicitly strove to create an anonymous crowd, and so did not indulge in artificial micro-action.[37]

For Tadeusz Kaczyński, Horowicz's contrasting of the oratorio-like quality of the First Act, played out in a gloomy half-light, with the 'romantic drama' of the Second faithfully conveyed the essence of the ideology of the work, although it appears that Witold Grucy's cheorography of the Bacchic dance, confined to a small group of dancers, was scarcely adequate to the task. The production nonetheless stayed in the repertory until 1971, and the Polskie Nagrania recording[38] provides insights into Mierzejewski's interpretation and the performances of the singers originally involved in the 1965 staging: Andrzej Hiolski (Roger), Hanna Rumowska (Roksana), Zdzisław Nikodem (Edrisi), Kazimierz Pustelak (the Shepherd), Marek Dąbrowski (Archiereios) and Anna Malewicz-Madey (the Deaconess).

During the 1970s several Polish houses took on *King Roger*, notably Opera Bałtycka in Gdańsk (29 June 1974), Krakowski Teatr Muzyczny in Kraków (19 September 1976), and the Teatr Wielki in Poznań (9 December 1979).

The first British production was mounted at Sadler's Wells in London in 1975 by the New Opera Company, which had been founded in 1957 with the express aim of giving performances of little-known twentieth-century works; its earlier successes included Schoenberg's *Erwartung*, Hindemith's *Cardillac*, Henze's *Boulevard Solitude* and Goehr's *Arden Must Die*. For *King Roger*, in an English translation by Geoffrey Dunn, the company engaged the services of Charles Mackerras as conductor and Anthony Besch as director. The sets were designed by John Stoddart and the choreographer was Sally Gilpin. The principals were Peter Knapp (Roger), Janet Gail (Roksana) John Winfield (Edrisi) and David Hillman (the Shepherd); the Archierios was sung by Richard Angas and the Deaconess by Amilia Dixey. There were only two performances (on 14 and 17 May) of this remarkably faithful interpretation, but thanks to the association of the New Opera Company with English National Opera, *King Roger* was seen again at the

---

[37] *Ibid.*, p. 179.
[38] Muza XL0250-1, released in 1965; *cf.* also the Discography, pp. 161, below.

Poster advertising the staging of King Roger *in Palermo, 1949*

London Coliseum the following year. On this occasion, it featured Geoffrey Chard (Roger), Felicity Lott (Roksana), Gregory Dempsey (the Shepherd) and Terry Jenkins (Edrisi); John Tomlinson was the Archierios and Shelagh Squires the Deaconess.

There was a wide divergence of opinion amongst English critics following the Sadler's Wells performance: 'M.C.' (Martin Cooper), the main critic of *The Daily Telegraph*, found the substance of the music 'indeed slender' though it was 'dressed with every conceivable sauce and served on the most exotic porcelain'.[39] Jeremy Noble in *The Sunday Telegraph* hoped that it would have 'at least some limited future revival', but doubted that it would ever become a repertory opera or that it could succeed at the 'very exalted level at which its composer aimed'.[40] Following the example of Polish critics fifty years earlier, he picked out supposed and not always likely influences on Szymanowski's 'bejewelled but overladen pages', among them Rimsky-Korsakov's *Golden Cockerel*, Dukas's *La Péri* and Debussy's *Le Martyre de saint Sébastien*. In *The Observer* Peter Heyworth went the way of British post-War progressive orthodoxy and condemned Szymanowski for failing to 'cross the great divide'. Unlike Bartók, Stravinsky, Berg and Webern, he was 'fated only to glimpse the distant shore' – but even Heyworth could not help but admit that it was an 'attractive score' and that whatever echoes of other composers' work existed, the work stood 'on its own feet'.[41] Such a tone illustrates well the dilemma facing many British critics of how to approach a re-evaluation of Szymanowski's achievement and reconcile it with long-held beliefs, often of an incurably elitist nature, concerning membership of the twentieth-century composers' pantheon. One of the more amusing, and revealing, remarks came in a generally favourable review in *The Guardian* from Philip Hope-Wallace:

> The notions conveyed are easy enough to digest ('Nietzsche without tears', said a wag in the interval). So is the music: accessible, I mean. 'One rather wishes it was less so', said another commentator.[42]

The production met with unreserved praise from William Mann in *The Times,* and the work itself was described as a 'splendid, distinctive contribution to our century's opera'.[43] Other favourable commendations came from Ronald Crichton in *The Financial Times*:

---

[39] ''King Roger' highly exotic', *The Daily Telegraph*, 15 May 1975.
[40] 'Too many tunes', *The Sunday Telegraph*, 18 May 1975.
[41] 'Routed by King Roger', *The Observer*, 18 May 1975.
[42] 'King Roger', *The Guardian*, 15 May 1975.
[43] 'King Roger', *The Times*, 15 May 1975.

a flair for handling rich and rare chromatic harmony and opalescent multi-layered orchestration with a concision and dramatic punch beyond the range of a mere dreamer. [...] *King Roger* establishes a potent atmosphere in the opening scene of chanting choirs in the Byzantine cathedral. Except for a flabby passage for the Shepherd in act 2, shortly before the dance, that atmosphere never loses grip.[44]

Desmond Shawe-Taylor, in *The Sunday Times*, described the First Act as masterly:

Ecstatic composers are seldom compact: but here Szymanowski succeeds in setting the scene and stating the contrast with forceful concision, and in moulding music and action into a beautifully rounded form.[45]

All three enthusiasts praised the theatrical impact of the final act, William Mann stating that Roger's hymn to the rising sun was musically as fine and satisfying as anything that had gone before it.

For the Polish musicologist and Szymanowski authority Teresa Chylińska, the Besch-Mackerras reading, which she saw at the Coliseum, was thoroughly convincing, especially in the way it linked scenic action with the flow of the music:

Thanks to this the staging was not a mere stringing together through the music of a series of operatic scenes, but a rapidly flowing music drama. The libretto was read psychologically rather than philosophically. [...] Interpreted in this way, [...] the staging [was] a truly theatrical spectacle rather than a static and monumental oratorio in costume. Obtrusive scenic literalness in the staging of the Christian, Arabic and ancient Greek worlds was avoided. Tension arose from the on-stage reactions and gestures of particular figures and groups. The shepherd did not voice ideas – he charmed his audience with them. The director's master-stroke was the Second Act, when the pious, intent, ascetic court of King Roger observed the entry of the followers of the shepherd: eastern dancers, clothed in ethereal, colourful garments, moving in time to strange, disturbing melodies. At first, the crowd looks on reluctantly, passively, with reserve, but then their resistance imperceptibly weakens, breaks down, and is eroded; tension rises as individual figures separate themselves, as if attracted by the magnetic force irradiated by the unknown newcomers, until at the end everyone is spinning around in the sensual delight of the dance and vanishing into the darkness of the night, led by Roksana-Maenad and Shepherd-Dionysus.[46]

---

[44] 'King Roger', *The Financial Times*, 16 May 1975.
[45] 'The king and the shepherd', *The Sunday Times*, 18 May 1975.
[46] Teresa Chylińska, "Król Roger" w Angielskiej Operze Narodowej' ('"King Roger"' at the English National Opera'), *Ruch Muzyczny*, 1976, No. 13, in Komorowska, *op. cit.*, pp. 185–86.

Andrzej Hiolski as King Roger, Warsaw, 1965

Since the New Opera-ENO triumph, *King Roger* has, alas, had to wait a further forty years for another British staging, though there have been magnificent concert performances, notably one by the City of Birmingham Symphony Orchestra under Simon Rattle with Thomas Hampson (Roger), Elzbieta Szmytka (Roksana), Philip Langridge (Edrisi), Ryszard Minkiewicz (the Shepherd), Robert Gierlach (Archiereios) and Jadwiga Rappé (Deaconess). It was given in Symphony Hall, Birmingham, on 17 July 1998, and repeated two days later at the BBC Proms in London.

The first staging in the Americas was at Teatro Colón in Buenos Aires on 8 November 1981 under Stanisław Wisłocki. Directed by Lech Komarnicki with designs by Andrzej Majewski, it again involved Hiolski in the role of Roger. Bożena Betley-Sieradzka was Roksana; the Shepherd was sung by Wiesław Ochman and Edrisi by Horacio Mastrango. In the same year Leonard Slatkin directed a concert performance in St Louis, but the first full production in the United States took place only in 1988 when it was put on by Long Beach Opera, California, conducted by Murry Sidlin and directed by David Alden. A less than enthusiastic review in *The New York Times* reveals that the production signally failed to introduce the work to American audiences, largely because it proved to be the first of a series of increasingly fanciful interpretations originating in a 'school of deconstructionist stage direction' flourishing in Europe, and particularly Germany, throughout the previous decade. The reviewer, Will Crutchfield, stated baldly that Alden was less concerned with a justifiable interpretation than 'often oppositional comment' which amounted to little more than inept experimentation:

> All the tired clichés of the genre were paraded in a jumble: studied ugliness of decor (white bed sheets represented the Cathedral of Palermo); business suits, raincoats, 60's prom dresses and dark glasses on the actors; unshaded white light bulbs hung from wires; a TV monitor on stage showing random security scans of the Convention Center of which the theatre is part; rolling on the floor; chalk-white faces; much play with shoes, suitcases and handbags; the whole shebang. All was drab; nothing suggested careful rehearsal or cogent argument.[47]

Tired cliché and dubious interpretation have, alas, become the norm since 2000 in European stagings, although the few American performances mounted since the Long Beach disaster have remained true to Szymanowski's general intention. These include the Bard Summerscape (Annandale-on-Hudson, New York State) in July 2008, where in an ambitious double-bill, *King Roger* was preceded by *Harnasie*, both in productions directed and designed by Lech Majewski with Leon Botstein conducting. Adam Kruszewski sang the part of Roger, Iwona Hossa Roksana and Tadeusz Szlenkier the Shepherd, and the chorus was supplied by the Wrocław Opera. Philip Kennicott, reviewing for *The Washington Post*, believed that Majewski took a huge risk in avoiding homoerotic references, contentiously stating that removal of the subterranean sex motif may not leave anything 'that makes sense in the 21st century'. There were minor misjudgements in matters of design: for example, fire and water were contrasted to underline one of the 'essential dualities that define the philosophical world of the opera – but the water dripping from a large inverted cone throughout the second act simply made too much noise'. Kennicott also questioned the directing of a bright light into the audience's eyes at the end of the work – 'a powerful gesture that has been used before, and too often, by other stage directors'.[48]

Opera Circle, a Cleveland-based company run by Jacek Sobieski and his wife Dorota, performed a modern-dress version of the opera in the rather incongruous surroundings of the First Baptist Church in Shaker Heights, Ohio, on 28–30 October 2011. But by all accounts, the finest recent

---

[47] Will Crutchfield, 'Szymanowski's "King Roger" in California', *The New York Times*, 26 January 1988.
[48] Philip Kennicott, 'King Roger, A Confounding Object of Desire', *The Washington Post*, 29 July 2008.

performance was a staging in July 2012 at Santa Fe, New Mexico, with Evan Rogister conducting and Stephen Wadsworth directing. Mariusz Kwiecien sang the part of Roger, supported by Erin Morley (Roksana), William Burden (the Shepherd), and Dennis Petersen (Edrisi). There was no intermission, ensuring that a sense of mystery and menace was preserved throughout. Though Wadsworth referred to Sicily's various cultural strands, he moved the action forward to roughly the period of the composition of *King Roger*, providing 'a compressed chronicle of psychological transformation', which culminated in the final moments when 'Roger's purified heart sustains both sacred and profane love in an overwhelming C major apotheosis'.[49] Thomas Lynch's designs hinted at Odilon Redon's symbolist dreamscapes, with a very simple depiction of the opening scene:

> just golden murals, rows of wood chairs and a glittering throne for the king. Nuns, clerics and noblemen in severe black garments enter, along with people wearing exotic northern African and Middle Eastern costumes (designed by Ann Hould-Ward). But King Roger [...] is dressed in a three-piece gray suit, though he wears a crown and wraps himself, almost protectively, in a radiant robe.[50]
>
> Kwiecien's interpretation was particularly commended: Anxious, fearful, incomplete, restless, he roams the stage like a desperate creature. I can't think of a contemporary singer who more totally inhabits a role in such powerful physical, emotional and vocal terms'.[51]

Recent European productions have frequently been sabotaged to some degree or other by their directors. Many of the clichés observed in the Long Beach performance constantly recur, betokening a marked lack of originality. Mariusz Treliński's 2007 version at Wrocław, with Ewa Michnik conducting, was something of a half-way house on the road to directorial mayhem. It was the second of his interpretations, the first production, notably more poised and visually striking, being mounted at Teatr Wielki in Warsaw in 2000. On this occasion, the conductor was Jacek Kasprzyk, whose interpretation with the same cast – Wojtek Drabowicz (Roger), Olga Pasiecznik (Roksana), Krzysztof Szmyt (Edrisi) and Piotr Beczala (the Shepherd) – is one of the best available recordings. The Wrocław production, which was exported to the Mariinsky Theatre in St Petersburg and subsequently the Edinburgh Festival in 2008 (with Andrzej Dobber as Roger, Elzbieta Szmytka as Roksana and Pavlo Tolstoy as the Shepherd), was infuriating as there were many telling moments, in spite of Treliński's

[49] John Stege, 'The Santa Fe Opera's King Roger stays focused', *The Santa Fe Reporter*, 25 July 2012.
[50] Anthony Tommasini, 'Caught between Desire and Duty', *The New York Times*, 27 July 2012.
[51] Stege, *loc. cit.*

'hauling the piece into dreary modernity'.[52] Modernity in this case involved back projections after the fashion of *2001: A Space Odyssey* with an apparently terminally ill Roger confined to a hospital bed.

A production by the Opéra de Paris in 2009 provoked extreme reactions. Renaud Machart likened the experience to 'a sort of acid trip that was systematically at odds with the libretto [...]. The spectator had to witness [...] the psychotic ravings of the director', Krzystof Warlikowski.[53] A review posted on the website 'Seen and Heard International' when the production was transferred to the Teatro Real, Madrid, in April 2011, referred to a staging that was 'inconsistent bordering absurd'.[54] There was even less connection here with Szymanowski's plot than there had been with the Wrocław and Mariinsky version. All the tired old gestures make their appearance – dark glasses, drinks poured over heads, and ineffectual operatic groping. For no obvious reason, a school-child, apparently the offspring of Roger (Mariusz Kwiecien) and Roksana (Olga Pasichnyk), appears just in time for the start of the Dionysia, initiated by Edrisi (Stefan Margita) with an injection in the king's arm. Finally, the Shepherd (Eric Cutler) is joined on stage by figures wearing Mickey Mouse heads, and the mice remain on stage doing gymnastics during Roger's final hymn.

The most recent presentation – before Kasper Holten's new production at the Royal Opera House, Covent Garden, in May 2015 – was David Pountney's for the Bregenz Festival of 2009, seen again at the Liceu Theatre in Barcelona the following year. The Bregenz performance – with the Vienna Symphony Orchestra, the Childrens' Chorus of the Musikhauptschule, Bregenz, Camerata Silesia and Polish Radio Choir, Kraków – was conducted by Sir Mark Elder to superb effect. In addition, the lighting was especially striking, and initially there was an impressive use of space and distribution of forces on a stage which consisted of rising steps, very like an amphitheatre. The production provoked considerable revulsion, however, for its interpretation of the final act and the sheer quantity of blood and gore. The burnt offering to Dionysus involved not the flowers specified by Szymanowski but the placing of bulls' heads at the foot of the altar, and at the climax of this scene, the Shepherd-Dionysus (Will Hartmann) cut Roksana's throat, before the crowd rushed off, leaving Roger (Scott Hendricks) to greet the sun.

[52] Tim Ashley, 'Dark gods triumph in the shepherd's boozy orgy', *The Guardian*, 27 August 2008 (a review of the Edinburgh performance).

[53] Renaud Machart, 'À l'Opéra Bastille, "Le Roi Roger" gâché par une mise en scène sous acide' (At the Opéra Bastille, "King Roger" ruined by a production under the influence of acid'), *Le Monde*, 20 June 2009.

[54] 'The Intentional Scandal: Szymanowski's King Roger in Madrid', Seen and Heard International, MusicWeb International (http://seenandheard-international.com/2011/04/the-intentional-scandal-szymanowskis-krol-roger-madrid-josemairurzun/).

After this rather gloomy survey of recent trends, one can only ponder whether Szymanowski himself, in spite of his declared disengagement,[55] would have been quite so eager to grant absolute freedom of action to director and performers. In spite of the huge expenditure of time, money, musicianship and technical ingenuity, audiences are little wiser as to the composer's and librettist's intentions.

---

[55] *Cf.* p. 140, above.

VII
Conclusion

King Roger is undeniably a strange piece of theatre, a mysterium that is not quite an opera, nor an oratorio, but rather something that is easier to define in terms of what it is not. As Henryk Opieński wrote after its first performance, its libretto is a 'dramatic poem in which there is no romance, no love duets, no murder, no duel, in a word none of those supposedly indispensable ingredients for operatic scenic "action".'[1] It is perhaps the inability to define its genre which has led to its becoming the vehicle for so many and varied concepts and interpretations, whether an opposition of religious dogmas, a homoerotic paean or a psychodrama tending towards Jungian integration. It is at least possible to envisage productions in which such elements are co-ordinated and kept in due proportion one to another, and proper account taken of the original plot and settings. It is only really in this way that the true significance of the work as a summation of musical traditions and European culture can be properly perceived. In musical terms it goes back to the very origins of the western tradition, drawing on plainsong and mediaeval organum, but also on compositional skills amassed in the course of a career which succeeded in merging a fundamentally Germanic approach (counterpoint and high-tension chromatic harmony) with one stemming from Franco-Russian models (orientalised melody, infectious rhythmic schemes and subtly variegated timbres). *King Roger* likewise embraces many and various strands of thought, ranging from the ancient Greeks through to the philosophy of the nineteenth century – the result of years of profound reflection which went into what became a matter of artistic survival for the composer.

The problems of establishing a genre (opera, oratorio, mysterium?) have no doubt led to recurring criticisms of *King Roger* on grounds of static action and the basic nature of its plot. Although it is undeniably as much a series of Russian-style tableaux, Szymanowski succeeded in adhering to a remarkable extent to essential dramatic unities. The action plays out over a twelve-hour time-span, and its focus on a single subject is comparable to that of other celebrated stage-works: *The Bacchae*, on which it is based,

---

[1] *Loc. cit.*

157

Tristan und Isolde, *Madama Butterfly* and, come to that, *Death in Venice*, to which in its positive treatment of the forces of Dionysus, it can be seen as polar opposite to Britten's ultimate statement of despairing negation.

In the end, *King Roger* has to do with vital life forces. The supposed stasis of its exterior action is offset by an animated inner drama, conveyed through the clash of ideas reflected in Szymanowski's increasingly turbulent score. The work progresses from the apparent timelessness of its opening scene through displays of mounting hedonism to the propulsion and take-off of the final moments with its precipitous rush to a grand C major resolution. So sudden is this arrival that the audience is left tantalised, on the verge of a new existence.

For Szymanowski, certainly, the completion of *King Roger* marked a definitive farewell to his old existence. As he realised towards the end of his creative life, he never again wrote anything comparable, since he was obliged to abandon his splendid isolation to enter the hurly-burly of life in the new Poland. In terms of his compositional activity, he was aware that the newly independent Poland required a new type of nationalistic culture, and as has been seen, he produced a number of works which differed radically from *King Roger*, particularly evident in the use of the folklore of the Polish highlands. He understood, too, that he had to justify his very existence in post-war Poland, and in the at times frantic struggle to support himself and other members of the family, he undertook additional journalistic work and eventually, much to the concern of friends and supporters, accepted the posts of Director of the Warsaw Conservatory and then Rector of the State Academy of Music. Although he left a valuable legacy in terms of both a considerable number of articles and his contribution to the foundation of an educational system which has largely survived into the present century, the price paid was a deterioration in health and a decline in the number of works completed. For these reasons, *King Roger* truly was a unique work, not only for Szymanowski but for European culture in general.

Select
Bibliography

Music Editions

Vocal Score (1925), piano reduction by Arthur Willner with text in Polish and German; Universal Edition, Vienna (7750)

Karol Szymanowski Complete Edition, Volume 14. Full score edited by Zofia Helman and Adam Mrygoń, with text in Polish and German; Polskie Wydawnictwo Muzyczne, Kraków/Universal Edition, Vienna, 1973

English Language

CHYLIŃSKA, TERESA, *Karol Szymanowski: His Life and Works* (transl. John Glowacki), Friends of Polish Music, University of Southern California, Los Angeles, 1993

DOWNES, STEPHEN, *Szymanowski, Eroticism and the Voices of Mythology*, Royal Musical Association Monographs, No. 11, Ashgate, Aldershot, 2003

SAMSON, JIM, *The Music of Szymanowski*, Kahn and Averill, London, 1980

WIGHTMAN, ALISTAIR, 'The Book of *King Roger*: Szymanowski's Opera in the Light of his Novel *Efebos*', *Musica Iagellonica*, Vol. 2, Kraków, 1997, pp. 161–214

————, *Karol Szymanowski: His Life and Work*, Ashgate, Aldershot, 1999

————, (ed. and transl.), *Szymanowski on Music: Selected Writings of Karol Szymanowski*, Toccata Press, London, 1999

English and German Language

BRISTIGER, MICHAŁ, SCRUTON, ROGER, and WEBER-BOCKHOLDT, PETRA (eds.), *Karol Szymanowski in seiner Zeit*, Wilhelm Fink Verlag, München, 1984

Polish Language

CHYLIŃSKA, TERESA, 'Karol Szymanowski i Tadeusz Miciński' ('Karol Szymanowski and Tadeusz Miciński'), in MARIA PODRAZA-KWIATKOWSKA (ed.), *Studia o Tadeusza Micińskim* ('Studies on Tadeusz Miciński'), Wydawnictwo Literackie, Kraków, 1979, pp. 325–40

————, (ed.), *Karol Szymanowski Korespondencja*, Tom 1, 1903–1919, Polskie Wydawnictwo Muzyczne, Kraków, 1982

————, (ed.), *Karol Szymanowski Korespondencja*, Tom 2, 1920–1926, Polskie Wydawnictwo Muzyczne, Kraków, 1995

————, (ed.), *Karol Szymanowski Korespondencja*, Tom 3, 1927–1931, Musica Iagellonica, Kraków, 1997

————, (ed.), *Karol Szymanowski Korespondencja*, Tom 4, 1932–1937, Musica Iagellonica, Kraków, 2002

————, (ed.), *Karol Szymanowski Pisma* ('Karol Szymanowski Writings'), Tom 2, Pisma literackie ('Literary Writings'), Polskie Wydawnictwo Muzyczne, Kraków, 1989

————, *Szymanowski i jego epoka* ('Szymanowski and his Epoch'), Musica Iagellonica, Kraków, 2008

IWASZKIEWICZ, JAROSŁAW, *Spotkania z Szymanowskim* ('Meetings with Szymanowski'), Polskie Wydawnictwo Muzyczne, Kraków, 1981

KOMOROWSKA, MAŁGORZATA, *Szymanowski w teatrze* ('Szymanowski in the Theatre'), Instytut Sztuki Polskiej Akademii Nauk, Warsaw, 1992

MICHAŁOWSKI, KORNEL, *Karol Szymanowski. Katalog tematyczny dzieł i bibliografia* ('Thematic Catalogue of Works and Bibliography'), Polskie Wydawnictwo Muzyczne, Kraków, 1967

————, (ed.), *Karol Szymanowski Pisma* ('Karol Szymanowski Writings'), Tom 1, Pisma muzyczne ('Musical Writings'), Polskie Wydawnictwo Muzyczne, Kraków, 1984

SMOTER, J. M. (ed.), *Karol Szymanowski we wspomnieniach* ('Karol Szymanowski Remembered'), Polskie Wydawnictwo Muzyczne, Kraków, 1974

SZYMANOWSKA, ZOFIA, *Opowieść o naszym domu* ('The Story of Our Home'), Polskie Wydawnictwo Muzyczne, Kraków, 1977

Discography

Polskie Nagrania Muza XL0250-51 (12″ vinyl) (1965), re-released on Olympia CD OCD 303 (1989): Chorus and Orchestra of Warsaw Teatr Wielki with Children's Chorus of the Polish Pathfinders' Union, cond. Mieczysław Mierzejewski, with Andrzej Hiolski (Roger), Hanna Rumowska (Roksana), Zdzisław Nikodem (Edrisi), Kazimierz Pustelak (Shepherd), Marek Dąbrowski (Archbishop) and Anna Malewicz-Madey (Deaconess)

Koch/Schwann CD Musica Mundi 314 014 K2 (1991): Chorus and Orchestra of Warsaw Teatr Wielki, cond. Robert Satanowski with Florian Skulski (Roger), Barbara Zagórzanka (Roksana), Stanisław Kowalski (Shepherd), Zdzisław Nikodem (Edrisi), Jerzy Ostapiuk (Archbishop) and Ryszarda Racewicz (Deaconess)

Naxos CD 8.660062–63 (1994): Polish State Philharmonic Orchestra and Chorus (Katowice) with the Kraków Philharmonic Boys' Choir, cond. Karol Stryja, with Andrzej Hiolski (King Roger), Barbara Zagórzanka (Roksana), Wiesław Ochman (Shepherd), Henryk Grychnik (Edrisi), Leonard Andrzej Mróz (Archbishop) and Anna Malewicz-Madey (Deaconess)

EMI Classics CD 5 56823 2 (1999): City of Birmingham Symphony Orchestra, Chorus and Youth Chorus, cond. Sir Simon Rattle, with Thomas Hampson (King Roger), Elzbieta Szmytka (Roksana), Philip Langridge (Edrisi), Ryszard Minkiewicz (Shepherd), Robert Gierlach (Archbishop) and Jadwiga Rappé (Deaconess)

Accord CD ACD 131-2 (2004): Chorus and Orchestra of Warsaw Teatr Wielki, cond. Jacek Kaspszyk with Wojtek Drabowicz (King Roger), Olga Pasiecznik (Roksana), Krzysztof Szmyt (Edrisi), Piotr Baczała (Shepherd), Romuald Tesarowicz (Archbishop) and Stefania Toczyska (Deaconess)

Narodowy Instytut Audiowizualny (National Audiovisual Institute) DVD 908259 554143 (2007): Orchestra and Choir of Opera Wrocławska and Angelus Chamber Choir, cond. Ewa Michnik, with Andrzej Dobber (King Roger), Aleksandra Buczek (Roksana), Rafał Majzner (Edrisi), Pavlo Tolstoy (Shepherd), Radosław Żukowski (Archbishop) and Barbara Bagińska (Deaconess); stage direction by Mariusz Treliński

C major DVD 702808 (2010): Bregenzer Festspiele, Vienna Symphonic orchestra with Children's Chorus of Musikhauptschule Bregenz, Camerata Silesia, and the Polish Radio Choir, Kraków, cond. Sir Mark Elder, with Scott Hendricks (King Roger), Olga Pasichnyk (Roksana), John Graham-Hall (Edrisi), Will Hartmann (Shepherd), Sorin Coliban (Archbishop) and Liubov Sokotova (Deaconess); stage direction by David Pountney

Index
of Szymanowski's Works

General
Index

165